WITHDRAWN
L. R. COLLEGE LIBRARY

880.09
M19c                    68646

| DATE DUE | | | |
|---|---|---|---|
| | | | |
| | | | |
| | | | |
| | | | |
| | | | |
| | | | |
| | | | |
| | | | |
| | | | |
| | | | |
| | | | |

GAYLORD M-2                    PRINTED IN U.S.A.

# CLASSICAL STUDIES

# CLASSICAL STUDIES

By J. W. MACKAIL

*Essay Index Reprint Series*

CARL A. RUDISILL LIBRARY
LENOIR RHYNE COLLEGE

BOOKS FOR LIBRARIES PRESS, INC.
FREEPORT, NEW YORK

First Published 1925
Reprinted 1968

880.09
M 19c
68646
January, 1970

LIBRARY OF CONGRESS CATALOG CARD NUMBER:
68-16950

PRINTED IN THE UNITED STATES OF AMERICA

# PREFACE

THE title of " Classical Studies" may bear a double
meaning; and it has been chosen in order to
indicate that both senses apply to the contents of
this volume. On the one hand these deal with
the classics as a subject of study and an instrument of education. They are not a defence of the
classics—for the classics require no defence—but
an attempt to set forth what the classics are, and
in what their value lies. We all, as has been said,
spend half our lives in misunderstanding one
another; and of the indifference or actual hostility
with which the claim of the classics to be an integral and irreplaceable element in higher education has been met, the main reason is to be found
in misconceptions both of what the classics are
and of what education means. For such misconceptions, classical scholars themselves have not
been without a share of responsibility. If they
are at all removed by this volume its purpose
will have been achieved.

But abstract doctrine, however sound, requires
embodiment and exemplification; and the volume
also includes a selection of classical studies in the
other sense of the term : studies, that is to say,
of certain aspects of the vitality, the unexhausted
interest, the bearing on actual life, of a few of the

great Greek and Latin classics ; of Homer at the
dawn of the classical civilisation, of Virgil and
Horace at its culminating point, of Ammianus
Marcellinus in its decline.

To these studies and addresses, which belong
to the last few years, has been prefixed the inaugural address given to the Classical Association
at its first annual General Meeting in 1904. It is
reprinted here, now that the Association has
attained its majority, to emphasise the fact that
the aims and ideals of the Association were clear
from the first, that they were the same then as
they are now, that they have been steadily maintained, and that they have exercised no little
influence, through troubled times, on national
education and national life.

My acknowledgments are due for permission
to reprint matter which had already been published in Classical Journals or Proceedings, or
as separate pamphlets, to the Councils of the
Classical Association and the Society for Pro-
motion of Roman Studies and to the Delegates of
the Oxford University Press.

J. W. M.

*August*, 1925.

# CONTENTS

# CLASSICAL STUDIES

## I

## THE PLACE OF GREEK AND LATIN IN HUMAN LIFE

An Address delivered to the Classical Association at its First General Meeting, held in the Examination Schools, Oxford, May 28, 1904.

The name of this Association, and the statement of the objects which it proposes to further, have reference to Greek and Latin as a single object of study, to be pursued by a common method, and with a common or at least an inseparable place both in education and in their bearing upon life. The ancient world, as it is summed up for us in the history and the literature of Greece and Rome, does indeed possess a certain imposing unity. But scientific research emphasises what is sufficiently obvious on a general view, that Greece and Rome represent two civilisations which, though they overlap and intermingle, though enwound and engrafted one on the other, have a different parentage, a distinct essence, and a separate product. Philology tells us that the Italo-Celtic family are but second cousins of the Hellenic. History shows a nearer affinity between the Roman and

the Teuton than between the Greek and the Latin.
The areas ruled by the thoughts and acts of the
two races always fell apart from their forced
or fortuitous coalescence.   The Greater Greece
beyond the Seas was temporary and fugitive, like
the New Rome on the extreme Eastern outpost of
Europe.  Each sank back into its environment,
and resumed the colour of the native soil and
atmosphere.   The Tarentine and Massiliot Re-
publics lapsed into the Latin world, as the Duchy
of Athens and the Principality of Achaia dissolved
into that nearer-Eastern world out of which
they were artificially created.   The Exarchate of
Ravenna ended its troubled and precarious life in
the course of nature, like the Latin Kingdom of
Jerusalem.  Nor is the difference in the art and
literature of the two races less radical.   The
sculpture and painting, the prose and poetry of
Greece remain something apart from those of
Europe; while the civic architecture of Rome,
like her language, her law, and her machinery of
government, became that of the Western world.
The influence of Christianity was insufficient to
bridge over this deeply rooted divergence, and the
separation of the Eastern and Western Churches
was only the formal acceptance of a more profound alienation.   It is not undesirable, when this
Association is being inaugurated, to emphasise
the difference between the two spheres which
classical studies include, and to realise fully that
they represent forces in the education and control
of life which are complementary, or even opposed,
to one another.   Under the ambiguous name of
the classics we include much to which the name
of classical can only be applied in different senses,

and by far-stretched analogies. The distinction, no less than the likeness, between the two spheres of classical study is of importance not only towards clear thought, but towards the pressing and practical question of the place which each holds separately and which both hold jointly in education, in culture, in our whole view and handling of human life. It is to this distinction that I would specially invite your attention, without trespassing upon any controversial ground towards which its consideration might lead us.

The classics, as an object of study and an instrument of culture, may in the ordinary usage be defined as all that is known to us through the Greek and Latin languages, or the knowledge of which is intimately connected with and inseparable from a knowledge of Greek and Latin: first and foremost coming the languages themselves, as mediums of the most exquisite delicacy, precision, and finish; then the literature embodied in the languages, as the original record of that history upon which our own history is founded, and the expression of the fundamental thought, the permanent aspiration, and the central emotion of mankind; then the effective surviving product of Greece and Rome in art, politics, religion, and the whole conduct and control of life. But the classics, in this sense, bear to us a still further implied meaning: that of a certain factor or element in our own lives, both individual and national, which depends upon and can only be expressed in terms of that knowledge. The classics are in this sense at once the roots and the soil out of which the modern world has grown, and from which, as a matter of mere scientific or historical fact, and

apart from any theory or preference, it draws
life through a thousand fibres.  In this organic
sense the phrase of the dead languages exactly
expresses what is not classical.  So far as they
are dead, they are not classical.  So far as they
are classical, they are alive, as part, and that
not the least part, of our own life.  "In our
life alone does nature live."  On dead letters
and arts, as on dead science and dead theology,
is pronounced the same inexorable sentence and
the same call to a higher activity : *Sine ut mortui
sepeliant mortuos suos ; tu autem vade, et annuntia
regnum Dei.*

On a broad survey of the facts we may say
that the study of the classics is the study of the
great bulk of relevant human history through
many ages, over a period of not less than a
thousand years, which is the bridge between the
prehistoric and the modern world.  We cannot
make this period begin later than 850 B.C., the date
to which modern criticism, reluctantly returning
to the ancient tradition, assigns the Homeric
poems.  We cannot make it end sooner than the
shifting of the world's axis by the growth of
Christianity and the emergence of Central Europe
in the third century after Christ.  But round these
thousand years extends a penumbra reaching
backward and forward for ages at each extreme.
Between the two great catastrophes in which the
Graeco-Latin world may be said to begin and end,
the sack of Knossos and the sack of Constantinople,
hardly much less than three thousand years inter-
vene ; and of the whole of this prodigious period
the Greek and Latin classics in their widest sense
are at once the key and the symbol.

In a more restricted and more accurate sense of the term, the classical periods of Greek and Latin civilisation are different, and stand apart. Each is confined within a space of little more than two centuries. The former begins and ends with the rise and fall of self-government in the free States of Greece Proper. The latter is included in the last century of the Roman Republic and the first of the Roman Empire. Between the two lies another period of equal extent, which is in literature as well as in history of great interest, but which is not that of the classical writers. We learn Greek and Latin in order to obtain access to the whole of the past; but still more, and as regards ordinary study primarily, to acquaint ourselves with these two classical periods, which represent in important respects the culmination of what mankind has done at the height of its trained intelligence as regards both the art of letters and the conduct of life. Arnold, in a well-known passage, states the case with admirable precision. "First," he says, "what a man seeks for his education is to get to know himself and the world. Next, for this knowledge it is before all things necessary that he acquaint himself with the best which has been thought and said in the world. Finally, of this best the classics of Greece and Rome form a very chief portion, and the portion most entirely satisfactory. With these conclusions lodged safe in one's mind, one is safe on the side of the humanities."

Such, then, is the scope and object of classical studies, such the place of the classics in a rational and educated human life. But the place of Latin and of Greek in such a life is in two spheres which, though they intersect and interact, are neither concentric nor co-extensive. He who truly knows both holds in his hand the keys of the past, which unlock doors in the house of the present, that *anceps dolus mille viis* far exceeding in intricacy the Cretan labyrinth of the Minoïds, or the maze of chambers and corridors that stretched round and beneath the palace-fortress of Blachernae. But these keys are two, and the doors they open are different.

The place of Rome, of the Latin temper and civilisation, the Latin achievement in the conquest of life, is definite and assured. It represents all the constructive and conservative forces which make life into an organic structure. Law, order, reverence for authority, the whole framework of political and social establishment, are the creation of Latin will and intelligence. Throughout the entire field of human activity, we are still carrying on the work of Rome on the lines drawn once for all by Latin genius. This Latin genius impressed itself most strongly on their grammar and their literature. And just as Latin grammar is an unequalled instrument for training of the mind in accurate thought, Latin literature is an instrument as unequalled for discipline of the practical reason.

While Rome stands for the constructive and conservative side of life, Greece represents the dissolving influence of analysis and the creative force of pure intelligence. The return to Greece, it has been said, is the return to nature; it has to be made again and again, always with a fresh access of insight, a fresh impulse of vitality. The return to Rome need never be made, because we have never quitted her. Rome we know. Deeper study, longer acquaintance, fresh discoveries, only fill in the details and confirm the outline of forms which, once impressed on the world, became indelible. Greece is in contrast something which we are so far from knowing that we hardly have a name for it. Even if accidental it is highly suggestive, that we can only speak of it by the name of one or another insignificant tribe, outside of the land we think of as Greece and of the culture we call Hellenic. The Hellenic name, to quote the famous words of Isocrates, seems not to stand for a race, but for intelligence itself; for an air of the spirit, that blows when and where it lists. At every point we are presented with its strange intermittence and elusiveness. What is Greek appears in a manner to have existed only to prepare the way for what is Latin, and then to dissatisfy us with that, lest one good custom, perhaps, should corrupt the world. The whirling nebula of commonwealths between the Aegean and the Adriatic took fixed shape merely as a burnt-out satellite of the *orbis Romanus*, the puny and eventless Roman province of Achaia. Greek art wandered lost through the world until Latin hands seized it and transmitted it to the Middle Ages. The Christology of the earlier Greek Church just fixed itself for a moment at Nicaea in order to hand over a symbol to the West; and the structure of thought built up by the Latin mind from Augustine to Aquinas was the central life of mediaeval Europe, while the Eastern Church lost itself in iridescent mists of supersubtle metaphysic. A history of Latin literature is a possible and actual thing—a thing of defined

scope and organic limits; as with the political
and social history of Rome, we can only redraw it
with a firmer hand and a greater mastery of detail ;
in their main substance and effect, the *Aeneid* or
the *Commentaries* of Caesar are what they have
been and have never ceased to be since they were
written.  The history of Greece and of Greek
letters has to be perpetually rewritten; in both
we seem to be dealing with something that is less
a substance than an atmosphere or an energy—
something elusive, penetrating, fugitive.  In the
sculpture of Phidias and his predecessors there is
a subtlety of modelling which actually defies the
pencil of the most accomplished draughtsman to
follow; the delicacy of outline, the fluidity of
plane, is like that of life itself.  So with the Greek
classics; they never yield their final secret.  Our
picture of the Homeric Age—by which I mean the
age that produced the Homeric poems as we know
them—is in constant flux; it is like a land seen
intermittently through dropping and lifting mists.
Modern scholars are revolutionising the whole
aspect and meaning of the Athenian drama.  The
work of Mr. Gilbert Murray on Euripides, and of
M. Victor Bérard on the *Odyssey*, to quote only
two instances, is of a really creative value in
reconstituting or revivifying two aspects of Greek
life.  We still need some one to light up for us
" Hellas and Mid-Argos," to give us a living
insight into that brilliant period between the
Median and Peloponnesian Wars when life
reached a sustained height and tension to which
history presents no parallel, and which yet is so
insubstantial and impalpable.  We cannot fix that
central time, any more than we can fix a central

place, of Greek national life. Where are we to look for the focus of that incalculable curve? In Elis or at Delphi? in the unwalled Eurotas valley, or where Athena lodged in the fenced house of Erechtheus? And where are we to seek the central moment of Hellenic culture, among those strange people, half children and half savages, yet so accomplished and so worldly, among whom were born beauty, truth, freedom, and vulgarity; on whom the mature mind of the Roman looked, as Egypt and Persia had done before him, with a mixture of fascinated contempt and admiring awe?

While Rome has laid down for us a realised standard of human conduct, Greece rears aloft, wavering and glittering before us, an unrealisable ideal of superhuman intelligence. It appears and disappears and reappears, always with the same extraordinary power of deflecting, dissolving, recreating the life that it touches. For a thousand years the Western world had to do without Greek —and it did very well; but there was something missing. Since then there have been three great movements of return to Greece—the later Renaissance, the rediscovery of Greece a hundred years ago, and now the fresh impulse that makes us face the problem again with our test-tubes and magnesium-flares, our armament of archaeology and history. In each of these cases the Greek influence has acted as a disturber and a quickener: "The men that have turned the world upside down are come hither also." It comes as something kindred to, yet transcending, our own habit of thought and mode of life, midway between our own Western inheritance and that of the alien

B

blood and mind of the East. The Indo-Chinese world stands now, as it has always stood, aloof and apart from our own. To earlier races in the valleys of the Nile and the Euphrates we owe the beginnings of science, art, and thought. From the Semitic stocks of the Syrian and Arabian plateaus we draw our religious beliefs, our chivalry, and our romance. The empires of Iran and Nippon have given birth to arts and civilisations, if not to literatures, of a high order of importance. But all these are foreign to us. Greece is foreign also; yet some strain of that remote blood mingles in our own. Using the Latin eye and hand and brain, we find in the Greek eye and hand and brain an insoluble enigma and a perpetual stimulus. Hundreds of years hence the same process of return to Greece may still be going on, amid a society still based upon the foundations and carrying on the work of Rome.

In the essay from which I have already quoted, Arnold observes that in the Athens of the fourth century B.C. we see a society dying of the triumph of the Liberal party, and in the age of the Antonines, a society dying of the triumph of the Conservative party. Notwithstanding the obvious criticism that Athens was ruined by Imperialist expansion, and that the decay of Rome is almost coincident with the era of peace, retrenchment, and reform inaugurated by the Good Emperors, the observation is interesting and suggestive. By which death is the study of the classics now menaced ?

The foundation of this Association is partly due to the general modern movement towards better organisation, more scientific methods, increased regard to efficiency. It is partly due also to an uneasiness which in some minds approaches terror. The classics appear before the world, not, as once, candidate and crowned, but in a garb and attitude of humility, almost of supplication. Scholars rally to the defence of a besieged fortress. Many of the phrases of half a century ago have become inverted. As the Middle Ages produced the Renaissance, as the Reformation produced the great Catholic revival, three hundred years of education based on Greek and Latin have produced the anti-classical reaction we see now. The supercilious attitude only too familiar among scholars of an earlier generation has been abandoned. It is not necessary to rush to the other extreme, and weaken our case by appeals to prejudice or to pity. No good will be done by calling names, or by ignoring facts. It is not thus that hostility is disarmed or that converts are made. In the first place, let us clear our minds of cant. Greek and Latin are not, as was once claimed for them, objects of study and means of education possessed of some mystical or sacramental value. That does not make them less educative as a study, less potent as an influence, but more. Nor need we aggravate the controversy, already sufficiently heated, as to the necessity of Greek and Latin at certain stages and in certain places of education, by involving it in an atmosphere of controversial theology. Into this matter I dare not enter further. The President of Magdalen, with tears in his voice, implored me not to utter even in a whisper a certain phrase which at present distracts this University ; and in any case I should not have been much inclined to pursue what seems to me a curiously confused issue. A controversy as to compulsory bread as an article of diet might conceivably be carried on with equal heat and pertinacity, were the supply of bread, and, let us say, of potatoes, in the hands of two bodies of highly educated persons representing enormous interests, and if the question were further complicated by one section of the disputants insisting that bread was not beef, while potatoes were, and another, that what was true of bread must be true of wine also.

Again, it may be stated with some emphasis that much in Greek and Latin literature is of no particular value, and its study has no appreciable claim on our regard. The brutal dexterity of later Greek art, the laboured pedantry of the Latin decadence, are objects merely for the scientific study of specialists. Even in the classical periods there is much of secondary value, much which is dead language. From this point of view Gregory the First and 'Amr ibn el-'Aṣi, if they were really responsible for the destruction of the Palatine and Alexandrian libraries, might be reckoned as unconscious benefactors of classical studies, and as having indeed inherited the practical sagacity of Roman administrators and the uncompromising logic of Greek thinkers.

Lord Cromer, who would, I hope, pardon me for quoting him as one in whom the Greek lucidity of intelligence is combined with the Roman faculty of constructive administration, once told me that he asked a lady at Cairo what she thought of the Pyramids; to which she replied, that she never saw anything half so silly in her life. "And I am rather inclined to agree," he added, "in this scathing but

original criticism." The contrast between this
modern attitude and Buonaparte's famous words
to his troops on the morning of the 3rd Thermidor
of the year Six puts very pointedly one side of
the contrast between the old and the new feeling
towards the classics.  It may be supplemented by
a more commonplace instance from my own experience.  I lately had occasion to confer with a
representative of the London Chamber of Commerce regarding certain examinations conducted
by that body.  He spoke of the difficulties arising
from the conservatism of school authorities; and
instanced the head master of one particular school,
not in any spirit of contempt, but rather in sorrow,
as "a man who had no soul for anything above
Latin and Greek."  The phrase is noteworthy; for
a real enthusiasm, not unlike in its nature to the
old enthusiasm for the classics, has arisen round
what are called practical studies.  Those which
specially kindled his were office work, typewriting,
and certain arithmetical processes called tots—the
last of which would very possibly have met with
the approval of Plato.  But if it were the case that
the soul had gone out of Greek and Latin, they
would be, what their opponents call them, dead
languages.  Or may the soul have gone out of
their teachers?  Have they lost the faculty of
making the classics alive, to themselves and to
those they teach?  For it profits little that the
thing taught is alive, if the person who teaches it
is dead.  To keep Greek and Latin from being in
effect dead languages, to keep classical culture a
vital influence, is the most important of the objects
which this Association has to promote.

The late Lord Bowen, in the preface to his

brilliant translation of Virgil, pointed out by a
single satiric touch one of the great weaknesses
of professional scholars.  They remind one, he
said, in their jealousy for the interests of these
studies, in which they seem to claim a kind of pro-
prietary right, of a timid elderly traveller fussing
over his luggage at a crowded railway station.
A life spent among the masterpieces of ancient
thought and art is, in fact, misspent if it fails to communicate to the student something of their large
spirit.  If with some scholars it results in something strangely small and petty, that is the fault
of the method and not of the subject of their study.
The fine vindication of these minute researches in
*A Grammarian's Funeral* is too well known to
quote; but the specialists are not always inspired
by so high an ideal.  The arguments for the value
in education of science and of modern languages
are equally applicable to the classics if studied by
proper methods and in a proper spirit, only that
they apply in a higher sense.  But the objections
which may be urged against science or modern
languages as preponderating elements of education
are no less applicable to Greek and Latin as they
are often taught and studied.  Two-thirds of the
study of the classics is vitiated by that very·
narrowness of outlook and over-specialisation of
research which is the defect of science as an
educational instrument.

But in spite of all that is said about the decay
of the classics as a main factor in education, there
has never been a time within memory when they
were as widely and as seriously studied as they
are now; and never a time in which they have
given promise of being a larger influence.  The

outlook upon life of the Homeric rhapsodes and
the Attic dramatists, the art of Ageladas and
Phidias, the thought of Plato and Aristotle, are
actual living forces of immense moment; and in
a like measure, though in a different way, this is
true of Cicero and Lucretius, of Horace and Virgil.
If they suffer temporary eclipses of fashion, we
may await the revolution of the wheel with confidence. Should they cease for a time—which I
do not think will be the case—to be an important
factor of education, time will reinstate them.
Signs of a reaction in their favour are already
visible. The State is beginning at last to take
the problem of higher education seriously in hand.
In any scheme aided and supervised by the State,
linguistic and literary training will henceforth
have its part, will neither be ignored nor squeezed
out. And if this is so, the classical languages,
each in its own sphere and to its own degree,
must, simply by the force of their own unrivalled
qualities towards imparting such training, assert
their place. After trying many substitutes, we
shall have to fall back on the fact that in Greek
and Latin we possess languages unequalled for
organic structure and exquisite precision, and
literatures which, because they reached perfection,
cannot become obsolete. We may get rid of cant
without losing reverence. The classics include
certain specific things which are unique in the
world, and without which human culture is and
always must be incomplete. These are the final
objects of the whole study which leads up to them.
Meanwhile, there is much to be done in quickening
the spirit and renewing the methods of classical
teaching, in lifting from off it a dead weight of

indolent tradition and class prejudice. If this is effected under the pressure of criticism from without, and of an awakened conscience within, the anti-classical movement may turn out to have been a scarcely disguised blessing to the cause of the classics.

I have ventured to place before the Association these general considerations with regard to the place of Greek and Latin in human life as a prelude to the more severely technical discussions which will be its main occupation. Here, in one of the ancient centres of humanism, where the ghosts of Dante and Erasmus move among more familiar shades, some such inaugural tribute to the humanities may not be thought unfitting before we set seriously to the work we propose to undertake:

As men in the old times, before the harps began,
Poured out wine for the high invisible ones.

## II

## THE REPORT OF THE PRIME MINISTER'S COMMITTEE ON THE CLASSICS IN EDUCATION

(1921)

THIS Report is dated June 7, and was published July 20 last. The eighteen months occupied by the Committee's investigations were not excessive, in view of the inevitable cumbrousness of procedure, the immense mass of the material supplied or collected, and the 140 witnesses who gave personal evidence. The ground has, for the first time, been fully traversed. The results are to be seen, not merely in the conclusions to which the Committee came and the specific recommendations which they make, but also in two facts of the highest importance. These are, first, that we now for the first time know (if not exactly, yet substantially) where we are as regards the position of the Classics and the machinery of classical education, and that this knowledge is accessible to the whole public; secondly, that the problem is set forth in its relation to the whole sphere and compass of national education. The final recommendation of the Committee is that the Reports of the four Committees on Science, Modern Languages, English, and Classics should be considered jointly, and that the elements of agreement in them should

17

be the basis for organising schemes of education both in schools and in universities.

The large public, who are frankly uninterested either in the Classics or in education, will not read the Report. What will soak through to them "by indirections" will not be the conspectus of the facts; it will be on the one hand a certain number of the *media axiomata* laid down in the Report, and on the other some portions of the practical advice given on the reference under which the Committee worked. Like all such reports, this one will be used as a magazine, out of which arguments may be drawn in support of views already held. It may be possible, if so it is most desirable, to set forth its substance briefly and yet with approximate accuracy, in a popular form, intelligible and even, perhaps, attractive to the plain man. At all events, all members of the Classical Association, whether or not they are professionally engaged in study or teaching of the Classics, can do something of the kind in their own immediate surroundings; and it is their clear duty to do so. For that purpose the Report must be studied and mastered in detail.

This paper is accordingly meant for preliminary guidance, *ad narrandum non ad probandum*. It would be impossible within its limits to analyse a document packed with matter and filling more than 300 closely printed pages. Even the summary of recommendations covers fourteen. The sections (Parts V. to VII.) dealing with Scotland, Ireland, and Wales must be for the moment set aside; and as regards the main body of the Report, all that can be done is to select and emphasise what seem the cardinal points. The definition and vindica-

tion of the Classics as an element in individual
and national welfare requires little or no comment.
The more detailed suggestions for extending the
field, increasing the potency, and improving the
methods of classical education require, and no
doubt will receive, a fuller scrutiny.

But first it may be well to note a group of
fallacies which vitiate much of both educational
theory and educational practice, for their influence
is visible in certain parts of this Report. One is
that boys or girls are divided by nature, and can
be divided for education, into two kinds—those who
have and those who have not "a capacity for literary
subjects ": as if language, the vehicle of all thought
and the motive force towards all action, were something "literary," and as if the object of education
were not to give the nutriment which creates capacity. Another is that "in schools where the pupils
must begin to earn their living at sixteen, those
subjects which have a direct bearing on their
subsequent occupation must have a special importance." That, no doubt, is true; but these
subjects (apart from manual training and physical
exercises) are the three R's, neither more nor
less. Everything else has a bearing just in so far
as it creates capacity. The suspicion of "vocational training" felt in the ranks of Labour is based
on a sound if a somewhat confused instinct. The
third is that education should be so planned as to
follow the line of least resistance. "Following the
boy's natural bent" is with a sounder judgment
condemned by Quintilian as fitted only for the
small proportion of abnormals, the *imbecilla ingenia*.

What the most cursory reading of the Report
brings out, and what its detailed study confirms,

is that Classics do not in fact hold a position of undue predominance in our general educational system or in any part of it; that, indeed, they do not hold any dominance at all. Given that they supply an element towards the intellectual and moral life of the nation and the individual not only important but irreplaceable,[1] the situation now, compared with what it was even twenty years ago, gives, so the Committee report, "ground for grave misgiving." "The danger with which we are faced is not that too many pupils will learn Latin and Greek, but that the greater part of the educated men and women of the nation will necessarily grow up in ignorance of the foundations on which European society is built" (p. 43). Modern pragmatism may contend that the foundations are there, and are not affected by our knowledge or ignorance of them. This is just the misconception which knowledge of the past, did it not exist, would have to be rediscovered in order to correct, for it is only such knowledge that brings home to us the fatal results of neglecting experience. In human life the foundations and the superstructure are not detachable, for they are constituent elements of a single living organism.

The facts, as ascertained and recorded by the Committee, are these: "In the Public Schools comparatively few boys are learning Greek." "Latin tends more and more to be dropped in the higher forms." None of the new Provided Schools have yet been able to develop a classical tradition.

---

[1] This could hardly be put better than it is put in the impressive concluding paragraph of the Report, p. 268. That is our case; we should only weaken it by bringing in secondary arguments, many of which are debateable and some (if we will be frank) are sophistical.

In nearly 1000 schools (those belonging to the Head Masters' Conference and the Head Masters' and Head Mistresses' Associations), with over 260,000 pupils, boys and girls, Greek is being taught only (in round numbers) to 7000 boys and 450 girls. The Report prudently forbears from treading on the hot ashes of compulsory Greek as an entrance test for the Universities. What it brings out, however, is how modern a thing compulsory Greek is. At Oxford and Cambridge it is a creation of the nineteenth century; in Scotland it only held good from 1858 to 1892.

Against Latin there is no wide or deep popular prejudice. Local education authorities are as a rule quite friendly to it. The general public realise that there is some use in it, and are even disposed to agree that without it secondary education is incomplete. But in the list of schools just cited a considerable number do not teach Latin at all; and in the whole of them little more than 2 per cent. of the pupils continue it beyond the First Examination stage. It is clear that if Latin is to be an integral part of secondary education, its study should normally be continued up to the end of school life. But it is also clear that, with more skilful school organisation from the earliest stages upward, pupils whose formal education stops at sixteen can easily by that time have obtained a good grounding in Latin, a fair ability in handling it, and a capacity for carrying forward or resuming its study later.

The upshot of the evidence on the minds of the Committee is to be gathered from their list of recommendations. These are unanimous; there are no dissents or reservations. A unanimous report, while not without the elements of weakness or ambiguity that attach to all compromises, carries great weight. True, it is made by a body all of whom have had "the inestimable advantage of an education in which the Classics played a conspicuous part," and of whom it may accordingly be suspected by hostile critics that (to quote their own words) "our view of the question is distorted by our individual predilections." But it means that within the camp there is substantial agreement. The Classics have suffered much from quarrels among their supporters or exponents— *nullas infestas hominibus bestias,* said Julian, *ut sunt sibi ferales plerique Christianorum*—and might be easier about their enemies if they could sometimes be saved from their friends.

There are in all fifty-seven recommendations, under eighteen heads. Their range is very wide, their relative importance very varied. A few will rouse sharp contention. A few others are only uncontentious because they are so vague. But four may be singled out as cardinal. Their significance will be best seen by their being set out in two pairs :

### LATIN.

*A.* Latin to be a normal part of the curriculum for all pupils in Public and Secondary Schools.

*B.* Latin to be retained or reinstated (as the case may be) as a necessary subject in all University Arts Courses.

### GREEK.

*C.* Knowledge of Greek to be required from all teachers of Latin.

*D.* Greek to be accepted as a universal alternative to Latin in all public examinations, and, "so far as possible," in all School and University curricula.

Of these four, the first three are the key to the whole situation. The fourth bears the aspect of a formula arrived at in order to secure unanimity. Is it a pious doctrine, or one meant to mould actual usage ? If the latter, it is not clear that its implications have been thought out : at all events, they are not stated. If the former, one understands why there is no suggestion that knowledge of Latin should be required from all teachers of Greek. Perhaps all it means is conveyed in the words (p. 121) "to secure that boys should be given the opportunity of acquiring some knowledge of Greek, and if they have no time to pursue both, of making the choice "—when ?—" between it and Latin." Perhaps we may let it go at that. Of Latinless Greek—Greek not interpreted, or as some would say, wrongly I think, diluted, into the terms of the Latin mind—we have too little experience to judge how it would work. It might act as an intoxicant, or as an explosive, or it might not act at all. Of Homer indeed this is not true ; but that is because Homer, to put it in the form of a paradox, is not Greek. Will any one be bold enough to revive the Roman doctrine and practice of beginning Greek with Homer? That would mean, of course, a revolution in Greek teaching.

To these four cardinal recommendations are to be added six others, the first five of which are all of high importance, and not only so, but are capable of being carried into effect by administrative action.   The Committee advise :

1. Organised transfer of pupils, with the co-operation of head masters and head mistresses, at an age not later than fourteen, from schools which do not to schools which do provide a full Classical Course.

2. Replacement of Advanced Courses by free combinations of advanced work ; or, so far as that may be impracticable, recognition of Advanced Courses including Latin (or Greek) alone.

3. Higher allowance for Classics in the Civil Service Examinations, both Class I. and Clerical.

4. Retention of all the existing provision of Classical Scholarships at Oxford and Cambridge, and increased provision in the other Universities.

5. Reinstatement in elementary education of the teaching of formal grammar, as the basis of all linguistic and literary study whether of the mother tongue or of any other language, ancient or modern.

6. "Measures to be devised by the Board of Education" towards giving Greek a footing, or preventing its disappearance, in schools.

On these a few observations may be added.

1. The question of transfer is full of difficulties. Without loyal co-operation on the part of school authorities, and cheerful acquiescence on the part of parents, the system could not work at all.   But even so, it is a desperate remedy.   It might even aggravate the drawbacks which it is meant to remove.   Break of gauge is in itself always awkward and wasteful.   A double break of gauge at eleven and fourteen is still more so.   Further, transfer from one school to another before the

First Examination stage would *pro tanto* dislocate
the whole school organisation, besides making it
more difficult than ever for the former school to
develop. Patience, and advance, however slow,
on a broad front are needed. But meanwhile a
provisional solution may perhaps be found in
encouragement of transfer at the First Examination
stage, and its discouragement earlier. This means
that for such pupils, at any rate, Greek will not
be begun before fifteen : and they would tend to
set the pattern for the whole school. But that
need not be an unmixed misfortune. If recommendations *A*, *B*, and *C* were accepted and made
fully operative, the study of Greek would be
begun with some marked advantages, and could
be both much more rapid and much more effective.
Between fifteen and eighteen Greek could be
mastered up to an adequate point : and these are
just the years in which it could be attacked with
the necessary interest and intelligence. This, or
something very like it, was in effect the doctrine
of the great humanists. "When they had herd
me speak of yᵉ greke literature or lerning," More
writes of his Utopians, "they made wonderfull
earneste and importunate sute vnto me that I
would teach and instructe them in that tonge and
learninge. I beganne therfore to reade vnto them,
at the first truelie more bicause I would not seme
to refuse the labour, then that I hooped that they
would any thing profite therein. But when I had
gone forward a litle, I perceaued incontinente by
their diligence, that my laboure should not be
bestowed in vaine. In lesse then thre yeres space
there was nothing in the greke tonge that they
lacked. They were hable to rede good authors

withoute anie staye." For confirmation of this
doctrine or prophecy, see pp. 122 and 175 of the
Report.

2. As regards Advanced Courses. They were
initiated as a war-emergency measure, for valid
reasons. They were expressly stated to be provisional and tentative. Nobody, so far as I am
aware, liked them much, or contemplated their
permanence. Much of the adverse criticism they
have incurred is due to ignorant or wilful misconception of this fact. Already, since the issue
of the Report, effect has been given to the second
half of this recommendation by the institution of
the new D Courses in the Regulations of 1921.

3 and 4. These hardly call for comment. The
former is welcome as a step made towards economy
and efficiency by substitution of induced for forced
draught. The only criticism to be made on the
latter is one which, while it is undeniably serious,
applies to the whole scholarship system, and,
indeed, to free or bounty-fed education itself.

5. This is directly educational, and of high
importance. The introduction of a rational and
simple standardised grammar as the basis of all
language teaching, while it would not work
miracles, would perhaps do as much as any other
single thing to ease the working and increase the
efficiency of the whole educational machine from
top to bottom.

There remains 6. Here we come to the kernel
of the Greek problem ; and here, unfortunately, the
Report gives no guidance. There needed no ghost
to tell us that the Board of Education should devise
measures for retaining or introducing Greek in
schools, or to express regret (p. 63) that "they

have apparently not thought it possible " to do so. But when we (or the Board) ask, What measures? the detailed recommendations of the Committee may be scrutinised in vain for an answer. We have to fall back on the cardinal recommendations; or, rather, on the first three of the four; for it will hardly be contended that Greek will be, to any substantial extent, either retained in or introduced into schools merely by its recognition as a possible alternative to Latin. But if Latin were required as an integral subject in the curricula of Secondary Schools and in University Arts Courses, and if adequate knowledge of Greek were required in all teachers of Latin, the naturalisation of the Classics in education would be secured. This cannot be effected immediately; it is idle to imagine that the situation can be retrieved by a stroke of the pen. But if it is a fixed and defined aim, continuous and accelerating progress can be made towards its substantial attainment. Supply will create demand, and demand create supply. Departmental regulations are little more than a codification of usage; but that little more may be all-important in directing movement. A generation hence, it may be hoped that usage, in both these matters, will be so general that it can, if necessary, be registered in enactment. But if this is to happen, there must be the most persistent and strenuous effort on the part of the Classical Association, not to cry its own wares, which is easy and useless, but to bring about further improvement in the spirit and methods of classical teaching, and in the qualifications to be looked for, as a mere matter of honesty and self-respect, in teachers of the Classics. The rest will be done by growing public appreciation of the results, in the product of the schools, of the strengthening, enlarging, and vitalising influence which Latin and Greek, or Latin alone, as taught by competent scholars to whom the Classics really mean something, can exert on the average boy or girl. Of this task it may be said in general, as Sir William Ramsay says in particular (pp. 190, 203) of the study of ancient geography, that "nothing has been done and everything remains to be done." Or if this be too sweeping —for in the eighteen years of its existence the Classical Association has done not a little—the path of safety and of honour lies in thinking nothing done so long as anything remains to do.

A large proportion of the working classes (p. 123) "are genuinely anxious to get the best possible education for their children"; and as to what that education is, most of them "accept unquestioningly the advice of the teacher." As has been said of them in another sphere, "they don't know what they want, but they insist on having it." When they do know, they will see that they get it. A free nation has the education, sooner or later, that it wants to have. "Where it is taught," the Committee report of Greek in Scotland (p. 221), "it is popular." In Scotland there is still some tradition of the humanist ideal. But even in England that ideal, only seen from far off in the sixteenth century, is beginning to take shape : *nec tam aversus equos Tyria sol iungit ab urbe.*

Very special attention must accordingly be given to the section of the Report dealing with matters of method. These matters are many and varied. Among them may be singled out for prominence the building up of a historical back-

ground; the choice and treatment of texts; the
place to be given to composition (on which there
is much more to be said than is said by the Committee); the moral importance of school libraries;
the use and abuse of translations; the scope of
what are called material aids; the so-called Direct
Method, on which an adverse judgment is pronounced.

The traditional method of classical teaching, so
the Committee conclude, while susceptible of and
calling for perpetual improvement, "has been
amply justified by results" (p. 276). But to save
it from slipping back into a dead tradition, it has
to be kept fluid; it has to be applied with intelligence; it has to preserve an open mind towards
change; it has to be worked, and that most of all
with beginners, by teachers of scholarly attainment.
And beyond all these, it has to be recognised as
an element in a larger system; and competition
between subjects, as a phrase and as a thing, must
be banished from education.

"Latin," the Report says (p. 40), "is suffering
unduly from the competition of modern and
scientific subjects." But Latin, and Greek too, is
a scientific and a modern subject. Have we at this
time of day to begin to learn that competition
between subjects is alike injurious to all the
competitors, and is founded either on a radically
vicious theory of education, or, what is nearer the
truth, on a total failure to understand what
education means?

The concordat arrived at in 1917—for which
not only the Classical Association, but the nation,
owes a debt to Sir Frederic Kenyon which
ought to be acknowledged—was perhaps the most

important step taken in education for many years. It got the educational machine on to the rails. All that is wanted now to make it run is motive force, common sense, and patience. The motive force does not come from Government Departments which release it, or from local education authorities which apply it, or from the teaching profession which uses it. It comes from the inarticulate but all-powerful national consciousness. But national consciousness, public opinion, can be formed; and now is the time to do so—now when all traditions, classical or anti-classical, are in flux. "One of the best means of assuring the position of the Classics in the educational system of the United Kingdom" is, so the Committee find, "that the membership of the Classical Association should be maintained and increased"; and twice over elsewhere they strongly urge all teachers of Classics to join it. Multiplication and strengthening of local branches, missionary work among the wider public, capture of the young, are named as specific aims; and the suggestion of the foundation of a Classical Institute, which should serve as the' headquarters of the Classical Association and of all kindred societies, will not escape notice. But something more is wanted than machinery. What will save, not the Classics—they need no salvation—but the study of the Classics, is, in the phrase which is perhaps the most significant in the whole Report, "the realisation that they have something to contribute to the problems of the present day and the permanent life of man." That this was so, used to be taken for granted as self-evident; then it was largely forgotten. It has to be realised and taught afresh. The ideal of classical education as an austere discipline must not be lost; there was never a time when it was more needed: but it must be linked up with and incorporated in the larger ideal of an enfranchised life.

One of the incomparable values of the Classics is that by their inherent virtue they supply the antidote against their own misuse. Before we set out to save the Classics, it would be well to make sure whether the Classics have saved us. Those who have really learned the lesson which the Classics teach will not feel either "nervous alarm" or "premature despair." It will not even seem to them particularly useful to have "grave misgivings." These are not the highest or the most powerful springs of action. The price had to be paid for old crimes and follies, entrenchment in privilege, supercilious detachment, obstinate resistance to change. So far as we shared in these, we must take our punishment. But *tristitia* no less than *superbia* is one of the deadly sins.

# III

# WHAT IS THE GOOD OF GREEK?

A Public Lecture, given at Melbourne, by the Invitation of the University, on June 22, 1923, Sir William Irvine, K.C.M.G., Lieutenant-Governor and Chief Justice of Victoria, in the Chair.

I may be allowed, on my first appearance before a Melbourne audience, to express my sense of the warmth of welcome which I have received not only from the University by whose invitation I am here, but more largely from the great capital of a great State, and from many of her most distinguished citizens. My gratitude is free from any of the embarrassment that might arise if this reception were a personal tribute. I recognise and acknowledge it as an expression of the kinship of the Universities of the Empire as joint members of the Commonwealth of Learning. And the presence of the Lieutenant-Governor in the chair emphasises the link between the University and the State. It is a mark of recognition that higher education and large humane culture are, no less than material prosperity or diffused comfort, matters of national concern : of determination that those "higher walks" to which Sir William Irvine has felicitously referred shall not be inaccessible to the citizens of a modern democratic Commonwealth.

If the subject chosen for this address may have seemed to any of those here, when it was announced, one of only sectional interest and irrelevant to a larger issue and a wider audience, I would ask them to suspend that judgment. For I hope to persuade you, if you need persuading, that it is neither.

I have put it in the form of a question. It is a question often asked in sarcasm or in scepticism, and even oftener in the mere carelessness that does not expect or wait for an answer. But it also may be, and is, asked in a spirit of serious inquiry. It is in this spirit that I ask you to consider it with me. The answer to be given is important; it deserves our best thought towards getting at the real truth of the matter. For on the nature of the answer, and the conviction or failure of conviction which it carries, depends our attitude as citizens of a responsible self-governing community towards the aim and sphere of national education in its widest sense. This is so in three respects : first, towards Greek as a language and a literature embodying a special manifestation of the human spirit ; next, towards that Greek civilisation out of which and under whose influence our own civilisation, as a matter of traceable and demonstrable historic fact, arose; and lastly, towards the whole group of humanistic studies of which Greek is one ; to the studies, that is to say, which are not concerned, or are not concerned directly, with the laws and processes of the physical world, but with life, thought, and conduct, with human nature as it is, as it has been, and as it may become.

Times change ; fashions vary ; beliefs alter.

In Scotland fifty years ago, when I was a schoolboy there, the question we are considering was
seldom if ever asked. The value of Greek was
taken for granted. Partly, this was a matter of
old tradition in a proud and conservative race.
Partly, it was due to the rooted belief in education,
the national respect for learning for its own sake.
Partly, it was the result of a more intangible
prestige, towards which these and other elements
combined. Education was prized, no doubt, for
its results in market value. But it was prized
higher, and more widely, for itself. It was recognised as enabling human beings, not perhaps to be
successful in the ordinary sense, but to realise
their moral powers and intellectual capacities ;
thus giving its possessors self-respect and entitling
them to respect from others, furnishing them with
a surer hold on life, with sources of lasting
strength and inward happiness.

In education as thus viewed, as given and
received in this spirit, the classics, and Greek in
particular, held a prominent and an unchallenged
place. With most pupils, the classical teaching
received did not go beyond the elements ; and it
was, of course, only a small minority of the population who received even that. But to be entered
on Latin was a source of conscious satisfaction ; it
was a distinction and a privilege. To be entered
on Greek was a higher and rarer distinction still.
Greek was regarded not as a useless luxury or an
idle accomplishment, but as a prize for the aptest
and most forward, who were a little envied, and
a good deal looked up to, by their less fortunate
schoolfellows. Nor was it a privilege in the lower
sense of the term, the appanage of superior birth

or wealth or social standing. That age was in a way more democratic than the present, because it was so by a common instinct rather than by contentious theory or abstract dogma. There were classes, and they were clearly defined; but they were organic. The artificial growth of class consciousness was yet to come. Class consciousness, and the sectionalism which it implies, are the antithesis of democracy, and they only hamper the life of a nation.

Such was the educational practice—it was rather practice or habit than theory—which produced a corresponding type of citizen: hard workers, clear reasoners, with developed capacities for acting and producing and thinking; with intelligence and character; people to whom life was a serious thing, and learning was perhaps the most precious thing in life.

Now we are in a new world. Nothing stands still. What we have to regard here is not the Scotland of fifty years ago, but the Australia of to-day. The industrial and political revolutions of the last century have been followed or accompanied by a cultural revolution no less profound. Great new fields of knowledge have been opened. There has been an immense specialisation of industry in the intellectual field. One of the most marked results of this revolution was that competition rather than co-operation of studies became prevalent. A multitude of options replaced the old unity of education; and vocational training was held of more account than the formation of a wide solid basis of intelligence and character. Education, or what went by that name, was given and received not for its own sake, not for its human and humanising value, but for its material profit, its immediate value in the market. As cause and as consequence, there came a marked loss of belief in learning as an end in itself, as an inward possession. With loss of belief in it there naturally came loss of respect for it in others, perhaps, too, of the self-respect it created in its possessors, and of the sense of human dignity which it once had given.

So it was that Latin and Greek came to be thought of, and then openly spoken of, as dead languages. Latin was kept, as it were on sufferance, for certain direct and indispensable uses. Greek tended more and more to be discarded as useless. The results of this were not immediately obvious, still less were they immediately fatal. We have been until lately living on the intellectual and moral capital inherited by us. But we have been and are using it up fast. That form of wealth, like others, becomes exhausted if it is not kept steadily replenished.

The object of the most clear-sighted thinkers and administrators is to reinstate, while there is still time, the ideal of humanism. That ideal is to realise human possibilities and rise to them ; to grasp and assimilate the fundamental truths of life ; to get in touch, by methods which call for perpetual readjustment, but on lines which remain steadily the same, with the human spirit and the human environment ; with the spectacle of the world in which we find ourselves, with the laws and processes of nature, and with the history, thought, and action of mankind.

Now the use of Greek is this, that it lies at the base of humanism. It was through the Greek genius that man became fully human ; and without Greek the humanistic mastery of life remains incomplete. And there is this further point to be added—it is of scarcely inferior importance—that the Greek achievement, more particularly in literature, both prose and poetry, is unequalled in quality. In the great Greek writers there is an excellence never reached before or since. They supply us, and this is as true now as it ever was, not only with an unfailing source of the highest human pleasure, but with a permanent model and standard for our own utmost effort.

Greek is not a quack specific. It can be badly taught and badly learned. It can be so handled (as all the best things can) that it becomes useless or worse than useless. But, even after all allowance is made for this, it is a gate opening into an enlarged and ennobled life. Education without Greek may be, and often is, very good ; but with Greek it is better. In this, as in other things, the hope may be cherished that this Commonwealth will not be content with anything short of the best. No democratic nation can fulfil the height of its mission unless it develops the highest possible level of culture throughout the community. No nation conscious of its own greatness and realising in what national greatness consists can afford to do without the highly cultured citizen who is of vital power in civic or State affairs, or the trained scholar whose function it is to keep up the quality and standard of culture.

Here a word must be said on the doctrine of substitutes. It is often asserted or suggested that the value of Greek may be got in other ways ; that through translations of the Greek classics,

and through modern books about Greek history,
Greek civilisation, Greek letters, thought, and art,
we can acquire all that is really useful or enlight-
ening for us, without the labour of learning the
Greek language. This is a complete fallacy.
However it may be in other matters, in things of
the mind there is no such thing as " getting ninepence for fourpence." Substitutes are futile :
short-cuts lead nowhere. The way can only be
entered through the gate. " I hope all will be
well," says that brisk lad, Ignorance, in the
*Pilgrim's Progress*, " and as for the gate that you
talk of, all the world knows that that is a great
way off of our Country. I cannot think that any
man in all our parts doth so much as know the
way to it ; nor need they matter whether they do
or no, since we have, as you see, a fine pleasant
green lane, that comes down from our Country
the next way into it." "It pities me much for
this poor man," Christian observes to Hopeful ;
"it will certainly go ill with him at last." And so
it did.

Translations from the Greek have their use
and their value ; but they can in no sense replace
the originals. This cannot be put more briefly or
pointedly than in the words of a distinguished
scholar and translator, Professor Gilbert Murray ;
they may carry the more weight here because he
is himself Australian-born : " When we translate
it, the glory is gone." That is true of all the
Greek classics, but eminently true of the greatest
glory of Greek, its poetry. It is of the essence of
poetry that it cannot be translated. The attempt
is continually made, because the lure is irresistible.
New translations go on being made, simply

because each, when it is made, is and is felt to be unsatisfying, misses the vital essence.

So, too, with books or lectures about Greek literature, Greek thought or speculation, Greek political theory and practice. To those who have entered through the gate they may be and often are of the greatest value. To those who have not, they may by luck be stimulating, but are mostly either useless or misleading.

During the Middle Ages, Greek was lost to Europe. Its re-discovery in the fifteenth century was equal in importance to the discovery of America; both were new worlds. There followed on their discovery, and largely as a consequence of it, a great liberation and expansion of the human mind. In course of time that movement, as happens to all movements of the human spirit, stagnated. Greek studies became professionalised, and Greek itself seemed to be losing some of its virtue. It did not; it was only biding its time. The new world-movement of the last generation has included what is nothing short of a new discovery of Greek. It is only possible here to mention in passing the enormous effect, not only on thought but on practice, of Plato's *Republic*, of the drama of Euripides, of all those historical or philosophical or imaginative writings which show us the Greek mind in speculation and in action. There is no ethical or political or social problem of our own day which the Greek mind did not raise, and of which, whether with success or with failure, it did not attempt a logical solution. One may say with conviction that the Greekless mind is as imperfectly equipped for citizenship as it is for appreciation of literary and artistic excellence.

This is beginning to be realised ; but only just in time.  For Greek had already dwindled away in schools ; and, as a natural or even necessary consequence, became very largely crowded out in the Universities.  There has been a lamentable falling off both in the provision for teaching Greek and in the numbers of pupils learning it.  This is what can be, as it ought to be, remedied ; it will be, if the public consciousness is aroused.  In Scotland, once a home of Greek study, the Education Department deplored, not more than a dozen years ago, that industrial communities seemed to feel no use for Greek.  This would hardly be said by responsible authorities now ; nor, if it were, would it be accepted by an intelligent democracy.  It is an industrial community which has special need of a high civilisation.

It is time now to say something about that Greek literature for the sake of which it is that we learn Greek.  But first it should be noted that the Greek language itself is an unequalled instrument for delicacy, accuracy, and beauty.  It was applied to many purposes by writers of all sorts ; the stream of time has brought down to us large quantities of rubbish as well as the gold.  But the language itself, even when used as it often was to little purpose, gives a new insight into the mechanism of expression.

The Greek genius created that language, and in it and by means of it created all the main types of literature, both in prose and poetry, and brought nearly all of them to perfection.  Further, in the hands of its great masters, it gave expression in them, once for all, to the primal and essential interests of humanity.

Those who do not know Greek must of course take this on trust; they can only prove it for themselves by learning Greek. And even those who have learned Greek cannot realise its value until they have had experience of life. There is a well-known passage in Macaulay's Diary where, after reading Thucydides (perhaps for the tenth or twentieth time) when he was himself a practised statesman and an accomplished historian, he adds, as comment on his amazed admiration, "Young men, whatever their genius may be, are no judges." It would be easy, but unprofitable, to multiply testimonies. But two more may be cited, as coming from men whose integrity of mind cannot be doubted, who took no doctrines on trust or in indolent acquiescence, and who held no brief for the Classics. Wordsworth calls Herodotus "the most interesting and instructive book, next to the Bible, that has ever been written." Mill pays homage to the Greeks as "the beginners of everything, who made the indispensable first steps which are the foundation of all the rest."

Herodotus no doubt remains both interesting and instructive in what is left of him in a translation. But the difference! the light and colour, the pulse of life, the live voice, have all gone out of it. What Mill had more particularly in mind was the sphere in which his own chief interest lay, that of politics, economics, and social science. Here also translations are quite ineffective substitutes. I have already mentioned the immense influence of Plato, the first and most advanced of Socialists, on modern social theory and practice, both among the Labour Party and in the general trend of popular thought. But that influence acts

D

mainly at second or third hand; and in second-
hand knowledge there is a very subtle danger.  As
diluted or distorted, whether by translation in the
ordinary sense, or by the still more perilous translation of substance, which whether consciously
or unconsciously is made by all who attempt to
popularise the unknown, Greek can become, as
the case may be, a narcotic, or an intoxicant, or a
high-explosive.  There is only one security against
this danger; and that is, to know Greek.

Another point may be made here.  The Greek
masterpieces teach us the lesson, never more
needed than now, of humility.  They make us
feel that we have to go to school to the Greeks.
Goethe said of himself in the art of which he was
so great a master, " Beside the Greek poets I
am absolutely nothing."  In a confused Babel of
tongues, in the torrent of cleverness which spouts
and foams round us in endless volume from
journalists, novelists, poets, propagandists, it is
through Greek that we can keep our feet on solid
ground; can realise the virtue of direct truth to
nature, of economy in language, of simplicity.
Crystalline simplicity—what tells and what lasts
—is the final quality of Greek work whether in
prose or in poetry.   In translations, even the best,
it evaporates or becomes turbid.   This is just why
I will now ask you to consider a few instances
from Greek prose-writers and poets.

Let us take first the account given by Herodotus
of Marathon, the battle which even now can hardly
be named without a lifting of the heart, which
determined the whole course of European civilisation, and fixed for a thousand years the
Western limit of the Asiatic races.   This is how

Herodotus, in a few simple sentences, tells the story; I translate his Greek as literally, word for word, as I can.

"Then the Athenians were let go, and charged the barbarians at a run. Between the two armies was a mile or rather more. The Persians, seeing them coming on at a run, prepared to receive them, imputing to the Athenians nothing short of disastrous insanity when they saw them few, and even so coming on at a run, with no force of cavalry or archers. So the barbarians thought. But the Athenians, when they engaged the barbarians in close order, fought worthily of account. The first of all Greeks within our knowledge they charged an enemy at a run; the first they stood the sight of the Median uniform and the men who wore it; until then the very name of the Medians was a terror to Greeks to hear. The fighting at Marathon lasted a long time. In the centre of the line the barbarians had the advantage, where the Persians themselves and the Sacians were posted; there the barbarians had the advantage, broke the line, and began to pursue inland. But on each wing the Athenians and Plateans won. As they won, they left the routed forces of the barbarians to flee, and bringing both wings together, engaged those who had broken their centre; and the Athenians won, and pursued the fleeing Persians, cutting them down, until they reached the sea."

That is all. In this or in any English it is bald. That is just my point. In the Greek, the simplicity is charged with emotion that makes every word tell; and it cannot be read, for the first or for the hundredth time, without a thrill of exaltation and awe.

Turn now from Herodotus, "the father of history," to Thucydides, the earliest and still the

greatest of scientific historians, and look at the two
or three tense vivid pages giving the account of
the destruction of the great Athenian army in
Sicily.  " The modern historian," as Grote observes
when he reaches this episode in his History of
Greece, "strives in vain to convey the impression
of it which appears in the condensed and burning
phrases of Thucydides."  "There is no prose composition in the world which I place so high; it is
the *ne plus ultra* of human art": so Macaulay writes
of it, citing with delighted approval the comment
made on it by the poet Gray, "Is it or is it not the
finest thing you ever read in your life?"  We
can realise it now even better than they, when
we think of Gallipoli.  At Syracuse there were a
hundred and ten Athenian warships and about
forty thousand troops, the flower of Athens: and
this was out of a total population, slaves included,
of only half a million.  Imagine, if you can bear to
imagine it, the total loss both of the fleet—for at
Syracuse not one Athenian ship was saved—and
of the whole army landed on the peninsula; and
then listen, so far as it can be put into English,
to the Greek historian's description of the final
scene in a disaster even more awful and irre-
trievable.

All the day before, the wreck of the army had
been struggling through scrubbed hills under a
blazing sun without food or water or equipment,
the enemy on three sides mowing them down at
close range.  At night they had to halt; some three
hundred men broke through and went wandering
through the darkness, only to be caught and cut
down by cavalry the next day.

"When day broke, Nicias began to move the

army on; the Syracusans and their allies pressing
them in the same way from all sides, shooting
them down. The Athenians kept pressing on
towards the Asinarus river, forced by the attack
from all sides of the whole swarm of the enemy,
including numerous cavalry, and thinking that it
would be a bit easier for them if they could get
across the river, and at the same time by their
distress and their fierce craving to drink. When
they reach it, they tumble in, no longer in any
order, but every one eager to get across first.
The enemy, hard on their backs, made crossing
difficult now; for, forced as they were to move in
a crowd, they kept falling on one another and
trampling one another down; some perished at
once on their own spears and packs, others
stumbled and kept falling in heaps. From both
sides of the river—it ran between cliffs there—the
Syracusans kept shooting the Athenians from
above, and for the most part while they were
drinking greedily and all bunched in confusion in
the hollow river-bed; while the Peloponnesians
got down after them and made a great slaughter
of them in the river. The water was spoiled at
once, but was drunk as greedily as ever, mud and
all, full of blood, and fought for by the crowd. At
last, when the dead bodies were now lying in heaps
on one another in the river, and the army destroyed,
partly in the river-bed, and any that struggled
through by the cavalry, Nicias surrenders to
Gylippus, putting more reliance on him than on
the Syracusans; telling him and his Lacedaemonians
to do as they choose with him, but to stop the
murder of his men. Then Gylippus gave the order
to take prisoners."

A little later, the two Athenian generals, Nicias
and Demosthenes, were killed by the Syracusans,
"against the wish of Gylippus"; not that he was
any more humane or chivalrous than they, but
because he had looked forward to the glory of
parading them as prisoners at Sparta.  The surviving wreckage of the army was driven into the
quarries of Syracuse, where, with no food but a
little flour and water, no shelter, no medical
attendance, packed close and dying like flies, first
in the fierce autumn heat and then in the freezing
nights of early winter, amid the "intolerable stench"
of wounds and corpses, "suffering all that was
possible to suffer in such a place," they were
herded miserably for more than two months, and
the wretched survivors then sold for slaves.
"Such," is the unimpassioned comment of Thucydides, "was the total destruction, fleet and army
and everything, and few out of many returned
home."

The story of Anzac has been not unworthily
told, but not told like this ; nor could it have been
told so well as it has been, if those who have
recorded it had not themselves inherited something of the Greek tradition, with its economy of
language, its lucid simplicity, its exact truth.  Two
thousand years hence, will it be a story that the
inheritors of our civilisation will be able to see
as though it were passing before their own eyes?

Or once more, take the closing passage of
Plato's *Phaedo*, with its record, in which consummate art and incomparable beauty of language are
used with the amazing Greek simplicity, of the
last moments of Socrates.

"He uncovered his face, for he had covered

himself up, and said (they were his last words), 'Crito, I owe a cock to Asclepius; will you remember to pay the debt?' 'The debt shall be paid,' said Crito; 'is there anything else?' There was no answer to this question; but in a minute or two a movement was heard, and the attendants uncovered him; his eyes were set, and Crito closed his eyes and mouth.

"Such was the end, Echecrates, of our friend, whom I may truly call the wisest and justest and best of all the men whom I have ever known."

The quietness can be felt; the voice that does not need to shout in order to be heard. But no less here than in the other passages, the English can give but a faint idea of the lucid precision and effortless power of the Greek. This is still more so if we turn from prose to poetry, in which form and substance are wholly inseparable. Any instances from poetry had better, therefore, be of the briefest.

For one instance, I ask you to take the last line of the *Iliad*, "So these held funeral for Hector the knight," and the comment made on it by one of its translators who was himself a poet. "I cannot take my leave of this noble poem," are Cowper's words, "without expressing how much I am struck with this plain conclusion of it. . . . I recollect nothing among the works of mere man that exemplifies so strongly the true style of great antiquity." "The true style": that is a phrase worth remembering and taking to heart. For *le style*, in the famous adage of Buffon, *c'est l'homme même;* and when we speak of the true style we mean the perfect expression of the true greatness of man.

For another, one might cite what is perhaps the noblest utterance ever placed in human lips, the couplet written by Simonides for the memorial stone set up over the three hundred Spartans who died at Thermopylae : *Passer-by, tell the Lacedaemonians that we lie here obeying their orders.* So we may attempt to render it ; but this or any other rendering loses not only the beauty but half the meaning of the original. The word translated " passer-by " means that, but it also means " stranger," and it also means " friend." The word translated " lie " means that, but it also means " fell." The phrase rendered " obeying their orders " is many-faceted ; it means that, but it means likewise " accepting their laws " and " having faith in their word."

For another still, we might take one of the fragments of Sappho, that incomparable lyrist who was to the Greeks simply " the poetess " as Homer was " the poet ": the seven incredibly simple words, for instance, of which the English shadow is, " I loved you once, Atthis, long ago," and which give, as no other poet has given, the nightingale note with its liquid, piercing sweetness.

Or, if time allowed, I could speak of those many intense and poignant lines in Sophocles (the most consummate of all dramatists) that are not led up to and are not stressed, but simply are there as if they happened—lines in which language becomes transfigured and almost more than human. But of these one may gather some idea from lines in Shakespeare which have the same terrible and piercing simplicity, like Macduff's words in *Macbeth :*

I cannot but remember such things were,

or Edgar's in *King Lear:*

> Men must endure
> Their going hence, even as their coming hither.

In such lines, more than ever, the actual form, the music and cadence of the language, are of the essence of what the words express.  Translation spoils them ; commentary only blurs them.  The fact, then, is this: if we would make Greek poetry a possession and an inspiration of our own (and there is no possession more precious, no inspiration more powerful) we must know Greek.  There is no other way.

It is further to be borne in mind that Greek is at the foundation not only of literature and art and thought, not only of the physical and social sciences, but of the Christian religion.  It was, in fact, taught and learned in Europe from the sixteenth century onward primarily as the necessary equipment of clerics and theologians.  St. Paul is in this sense one of the most important Greek classics.  No less are the Gospels ; for while they are based on Aramaic documents or oral traditions, these are lost, and we cannot, except imperfectly and conjecturally, get behind the Greek Gospels. With St. Paul as with Plato, with St. Luke as with Herodotus, the English rendering inevitably loses something of the original by distortion or variation or subtle changes of implication or emphasis.  Both the Authorised and the Revised Versions, and any other that can be made, are necessarily imperfect.  I need not enlarge on this ; it is only necessary to note that Greek is indispensable for an educated ministry, and that it cannot be satisfactorily acquired in Universities

or theological colleges without school-grounding.
Colleges must be fed with prepared material if
they are to fulfil their own function. It is the bed-
rock principle of national education that it should
be a single organism, of which every part performs
its own function. In that organism, the Universities have the function, the Schools theirs. There
must be continuity, but not confusion. To set a
University to do the work of a secondary school
is as wasteful as it would be to set a secondary
school to do the work of a University. This
applies to Greek as it does to English or to
history or to science.

It has been noted by a thoughtful observer, as
the great weakness of American civilisation, that
there is no aspiration, in cities or communities, to
intellectual leadership; that the rivalry which is a
powerful and need not be an ignoble stimulus to
progress extends only to growth of numbers, or
material wealth, or industrial output. Is this true
of Australia also ? or of Melbourne? I hope not :
but the question must be asked expressly and
answered honestly. A White Australia worthy
of the name must be white not only racially but
culturally; it must preserve and heighten its
standards. People here, as in Great Britain, talk,
hopefully or despairingly as the case may be,
about the prospect of saving Greek. They have
done so for long. It is nearly fifty years since
Jowett wrote of Oxford and Cambridge : " I hope
we shall save Greek in the Universities." The
Universities cannot save either Greek or anything
else, unless they have national consciousness
behind them ; unless there is in the body of the
nation the will to live a high life, love and respect

for knowledge, belief in the discipline and elevating power of learning, a sense of the human ideal as it was created in Greece.

That ideal hinges on three words: truth, beauty, freedom. We have still to go back to Greece to learn savingly the lesson that these three are one and inseparable; that truth without beauty and freedom is a withering up of vitality; that beauty without truth and freedom is poisonous; that freedom without truth and beauty leads straight to anarchy and dissolution. Or, to put it in other words, it is only truth and beauty that make man free; it is only truth and freedom that make life beautiful; it is only beauty and freedom that make truth live.

I have shown, as I hope, that Greek is not an idle luxury. The heavier charge is that it is, or may be, an intoxicant. But that is true, as I have also endeavoured to indicate, of its dilutions and misinterpretations rather than of itself. Itself it is indeed a powerful stimulant, but also a disciplining and controlling power.

Still, one objection may be raised, and it is perhaps the commonest: what is the good of a little Greek? When science was introduced into our schools it was decried by reactionary conservatives as smattering. It has lived through that outcry and established itself. Now the tables are turned, and contempt is poured as freely (and as foolishly) on "a smattering of Greek and Latin." But smattering is a different thing from grounding. No one says that to learn the multiplication table is to get a smattering of arithmetic. To the question, What is the good of a little Greek? it would be sufficient answer that virtue

goes out from even a little of it. It is wonderful
how soon we can get into touch with the essence
of the Greek spirit even by touching a corner of
it, the hem of its garment. We forget it all afterwards? Perhaps; but it has made us different.
But the question itself, if we think a little more
deeply, is futile. What is the good, one might as
well ask, of a little of anything? of a little food?
or of a little joy? or, if we come to that, of a
little life? Life, with its splendour and its awful
brevity, is given us not to be left empty, but to
be filled. Even a very little Greek—but need it
be always so very little?—helps towards this,
whether we regard it as an instrument, or an
equipment, or an organic energy assimilated by
us and becoming part of us. It enables us to
enter more fully into the human inheritance.

I have touched on what Greek literature means,
but said nothing of Greek art; nor does the
occasion permit of our entering now on another
field of equally fascinating interest : what we owe,
not only historically and as a debt of the past,
but in actual research of the present day, to the
work of Greek masters in the mathematical and
physical sciences, and in the whole group of studies
which circle round the medical profession and the
mistress-art of healing. It must suffice if I have
shown, as has been my aim, that Greek is an
invaluable element in civilised life. If that be
established, it follows without argument that it is
an irreplaceable element in the education of a
civilised State.

What is civilisation? The word, like so many
in our language (sixty per cent., it has been calculated), is Latin; and the thing is in its substantial

structure a Latin achievement. But to the Romans, as to us, vital force came from Greece. They gained, as we do, experience, ideals, power of expression, sense of the dignity of human nature, from the products of the Greek genius. From the same source they drew their maxims on the relation of the individual to the community, and the relation of both individual and community to the physical world in which they live, and to the spiritual world which is the highest reality.

There is an old story, familiar no doubt to many here, of the question which I took for the title of this address being asked of a Dean of Christ Church a century ago or more, and of his reply that knowledge of Greek not only enabled those who possessed it to feel conscious superiority over others, but also led to positions of great dignity and emolument. The latter of these motives cannot be offered now; but there remains as a reward the dignity of human nature, and the spiritual emolument which cannot depreciate, cannot be lost or confiscated. For the former, the claim which holds good is that Greek makes us consciously superior not to others, but to ourselves. The good of Greek, in the last resort, is that it gives, in a way that nothing else quite does, the highest kind of joy; and such joys are not so common that we can afford to cast them away.

# IV

## PENELOPE IN THE ODYSSEY

JUST two hundred years ago, Pope wrote, in the postscript to his own translation, "The *Odyssey* is a perpetual source of poetry." That is as true now as it was then; and even more so, because our means of being able to appreciate the *Odyssey* are much larger than his or those of his age. In spite of all translations, popularisations, commentaries, the *Odyssey* itself is for each fresh reader a new miracle. The study of one of its great central and vital figures to which I invite you will have fulfilled its purpose if it sends those of you who have learnt or are learning Greek to Homer, and if it arouses, in those who have not, desire to drink at the fountain themselves. One word of warning, which is never superfluous, must be given; to listen to lectures is not to study the Classics; nor is it any substitute for that study.

Penelope is one of the great women of history. If at first sight she seems remote from, or even contrary to, modern ideals, a larger and more intelligent view will alter that misconception. She will reveal herself as no obsolete type, but as an individual figure, of extraordinary fineness and complexity, and intensely human because portrayed, or created, by a consummate artist.

In a sense, she has become obscured by her

own fame. She is universally known, but in a slovenly, superficial way. From being typical, she has tended to dwindle into a mere type, part of the defaced currency passed on from hand to hand. The type, as thus degraded, is that of the housewife—bloodless, tearful, incompetent, occupied in endless complainings and everlasting needlework. *Domum servavit, lanam fecit*, the phrase of one of the noblest and most touching of Roman epitaphs, has become debased, for her as for others, into a sort of sneer : into a description of the woman without brains, who must be always clinging and whose constancy is habit, not virtue.

The first touch of this—for it is no new thing —comes in the *Odyssey* itself; in the half-mocking, half-angry spurt of jealousy with which Calypso speaks of her. It is answered there by the grave and beautiful reply of Odysseus. But always afterwards it has tended to recur with aggravations. It is fully developed in Bacon's cynical sentence in the essay "Of Marriage and Single Life ": "Grave natures, led by custom, and therefore constant, are commonly loving husbands, as was said of Ulysses, *Vetulam suam praetulit immortalitati.*" On this it may be noted, first, that it was not said ; the words to which Bacon alludes were said not of Penelope, but of the "little nest among the rocks," his own island of Ithaca ; secondly, that it is dishonouring alike to Homer and to humanity ; and thirdly that *vetula*, "old woman," is a wilful falsification. The whole thing is an instance of the Elizabethan vulgarity which is so constantly mixed up with high thought and splendid imagination in that age. But all that

makes it still more worth while to get back to the
real Penelope, the Penelope of Homer.

The real Penelope? some one may say; one
of the great women of history? Surely you
mean, not of history, but of poetry? Here we
touch on the secret of art. Whether the actual
Penelope ever lived at all—probably she did—
does not matter. It would not make her less
real if she were as much of an imaginative invention as the Bradamante of Ariosto; nor more
real, if she were presented with the same minute
historical accuracy as the Gudrun of the Lax-
daela-saga. Poetry is the highest and ultimate
expression towards which history is perpetually
reaching.

Further, there is more in poetry (as one might
state the case) than the poet put there, that is,
than he consciously meant or planned. In some
of the detail which follows in this sketch, you may
reasonably ask, But did Homer have this in his
mind? The answer is, Yes and No. He certainly
did not, in the sense of a set of data on which he
worked, but vital creation from within outwards
has an instinctive or "inspired" knowledge. The
poet tells "what the Muses teach him." Think of
all the implied background to Hamlet, say, or to
Imogen. They are so real, so living, that they
create all round them a sort of world of reality, or
if we prefer to say so, of super-reality. Not only
do they exist, but their detailed environment exists,
takes shape, comes alive.

Those who read and delight in the *Odyssey*
as a masterpiece of poetry are often, and very
naturally, so enthralled by its fascination as a
story, its splendour of construction and brilliance

of handling, that they fail to appreciate fully other qualities no less remarkable, its subtle psychology, its pathos and humour, its insight into the springs of human nature. The best Greek art—and in this respect at least, Homer is thoroughly Greek —is so delicate, so reserved, so free from insistence and display, that it only yields its secret to the most careful study and to a corresponding fineness of apprehension. We feel its beauty, its charm, its magic potency; but we feel all these indistinctly. Even to handle it seems sometimes a sort of profanation. Art cannot be explained, any more than it can be analysed. But at least we may attempt to appreciate it better. And that is not hard. "Nature, purity, perspicacity, and simplicity," in the fine words which I quote again from Pope, "never walk in the clouds; they are obvious to all capacities, and where they are not evident, they do not exist."

One of the foolish things said in antiquity about the *Odyssey* was that Homer composed it for women after composing the *Iliad* for men. One of the foolish things said about it by a brilliant but eccentric modern writer was that it was written by a woman. What originated notions like these is the large part played in it by women. That marvellous picture-gallery includes half a dozen figures of the first rank, fully and finely drawn; Circe and Calypso, Arete and Nausicaa, Helen, Eurycleia (several of these, Helen and Arete especially, have outstanding gifts of capacity and intellect), but above all, Penelope herself. Round her, and her relation to Odysseus and Telemachus, the whole poem circles. From her first appearance in the Hall

E

at Ithaca in Book I., where the keynote is firmly
struck in the phrases by which she is introduced
—περίφρων Πηνελόπεια, δῖα γυναικῶν—to the final re-
union in Book XXIII., we are never allowed to
forget her.  She passes in and out of the scene
like a phrase in music or a gold thread in a woven
texture.  Gradually, as we study the poem more
closely and let its poetry sink into us, she takes
shape as a creation largely and delicately modelled,
extraordinarily true to life, fascinating alike in her
strength and weakness, and like a character of
Shakespeare's in the way that she is created from
within, vitally.

First, then, who was Penelope?  What is the
background of facts, as one might say, upon which
the artist produces his living figure?  We may
neglect here all the odds and ends of local tradition
or antiquarian invention; for we cannot say
whether, or how far, any of them belonged to the
story as it was known to the poet, and there is
nothing more dangerous than to read them into
the poem.

Of her own family we learn this from the
*Odyssey* itself: her father Icarius is still alive somewhere on the mainland; and she has brothers,
who are only mentioned once, casually; both
father and brothers are outside of the story.  She
has also a sister Iphthime, married to Eumelus
of Pherae in Thessaly, far away.  There is no
mention of her mother.  This much is stated in
the poem itself: but we may add to it another
very important fact, from the general and unvary-
ing main outlines of the heroic cycle, as they had
already become fixed before the age of Homer:
namely, that Icarius was the brother of Tyndareus,

and hence that Penelope is first cousin of Helen and Clytemnestra. This is in a sense the key to the whole structure of the poem.

From her home overseas she was married young to Odysseus. Telemachus was a newborn baby when Odysseus went to Troy : and the return is uniformly spoken of as in the twentieth year. Consequently when the action of the *Odyssey* opens he is nineteen, and she, if she married at fifteen, would be thirty-five or thirty-six—in any case, under forty, and at the "dangerous age." She is still in mature and unimpaired beauty, which is overpowering in its splendour whenever she can throw off the weight of anxiety and cloud of gloom. This beauty the poet leaves to be felt by its effects, without any formal description ; we do not know even if she was dark or fair, though the ivory-coloured face of XVIII. 196 suggests a dark complexion. When Athena has beautified her in her sleep—when, as we should put it in our more prosaic and unimaginative way, she is looking her best—the suitors cannot contain themselves for admiration.

But her beauty, great as it is, is almost eclipsed by a sort of impressiveness, mingled of skill, wisdom, and character. She is δῖα γυναικῶν, "the bright of women," but her constant epithets are περίφρων, "exceeding wise," and ἐχέφρων, "self-controlled"; a word which conveys the combined notions of chastity and of a sort of power held in reserve. The whole matter is summed up, early in the poem, in the magnificent praise of Antinous (II. 116) :

> —Athena has bestowed on her
> Wisdom of mind and excellence of skill

In beautiful devices manifold
Beyond all others, such as is not told
Even of those renowned in former time,
Achaean women lovely-tressed of old.

Eurymachus crystallises this, a little later, into two words, τῆς ἀρετῆς, "the excellence of her." No English, it may be added, can convey the magical beauty of the Greek line, τάων αἱ πάρος ἦσαν ἐϋπλοκαμῖδες Ἀχαιαί.

It is quite of a piece with this that she says she hates Antinous most of all the suitors; that young prince, though he had a pretty gift of speech, was something of a fop, and a good deal of a fool; and he expressed his admiration too openly. The plausible Eurymachus never imposes on her for a moment. Amphinomus was the one who pleased her best, "because he was quick of understanding." Herself she shows unusual intellectual power when she allows it play; but it has been stifled by circumstance, and the necessity of rigid and cruel self-control. She had but one passion, her love for Odysseus, and that had been starved: and her wisdom only made her feel her weakness and helplessness more keenly.

The position of a young wife left alone while only a girl in a strange house for many years was difficult at best, and became harder as years went on. Her mother-in-law, Anticleia, had been kind to her; but she was dead. Telemachus while a child engrossed her, with that jealous mother's love which often makes such difficulties when the boy grows up and begins to assert his own personality. She had her household duties, the needlework in which she was so accomplished, her poultry in which she took great delight (XIX.

537); the old family nurse loved her deeply;
Eumaeus, the foster-child of the house, "the man
who was loyal to his lords," has a real affection
for her. But she had no companions of her own
age, no real friends, no one to whom she could
pour herself out unreservedly. The burden of
her life became slowly too great for her to bear.
While the war at Troy went on, life was possible,
however anxious. But then came the slow sickening years of hope deferred. Anticleia died of a
broken heart. After her death Laertes aged
rapidly, gave up control of the house and buried
himself at his little country farm. She was among
old people. Odysseus' sister Clymene had married and gone to live in another island, Same.
The suitors began to pour in, treated the house
as their own, and became more and more intolerable, taxing all her wit and self-control to the
utmost. Except for them, it was a household of
women. Eumaeus was away at the hill farm; she
used to send for him often at first, but by and by
ceased even to do that. News was brought to
her of Odysseus again and again; it all proved
false. She was thrown in more and more on herself, on silence and brooding. Telemachus became
a problem: a sort of jealousy insensibly grew up
between them in spite of her love for him and his
real affection for her; it was perhaps accentuated
by his startling likeness to his father, which was
so strong that Helen at Lacedaemon, who had
never seen him, recognises him by it at once.
She felt the reins slipping from her; and her
control of the household, though she knew it to
be ineffective, was for her a sacred trust. The
policy of compromise she was forced into with

the suitors as they grew more insolent and masterful caused a chill of misunderstanding between mother and son; and neither of them spoke out. Even Telemachus must not take the place that she was desperately keeping open for Odysseus. She resented any attempt of his at self-assertion; she would keep him a child. For more than one reason she would not let him have any control over the women; indeed, the less he had to do with a young woman of the type of Melantho, the better. But she did not quite understand him; nor he her. When Antinous says that she is acting simply for her own vainglory, Telemachus does not contradict him.

This is the state of things at the opening of the *Odyssey;* it is all set out before us by delicate touches in Books I. and II. The fluid situation is precipitated by the visit of Athena. It is well to bear in mind that throughout, Athena, while a goddess, is also the inner god-prompted wisdom —the conversations in which she takes part must be read in this double light.

Almost in his first words Telemachus lets the unconscious friction appear. When Athena asks, "Are you really Odysseus' son?" his answer, with a curious accent of petulance, is "My mother says I am." And immediately after, when Athena has gone, and Penelope comes into the hall and asks the minstrel to sing another lay, not of the woes of Troy, Telemachus, apparently for the first time, snaps at her in public, and asserts that he is head of the house. He is finding himself, but, like a boy, is not very nice or considerate about it. She makes no answer, but slips away, disconcerted and astonished. After a night's thinking,

he announces to his nurse in Book II. his intention
of going to seek for his father. In his confidences
with Eurycleia one sees the mixture in him of
suspicion and tenderness: Penelope is not to be
told, really that she may not have any opportunity
to interfere, but also, as he adds in a mood between
malice and affection, ὡς ἂν μὴ κλαίουσα κατὰ χρόα
καλὸν ἰάπτῃ, "that she may not spoil her lovely
complexion with crying."

So he slips off in the night; and the next of
Penelope is when she hears of his being gone
from Medon the herald. This scene, and the
episode of Penelope's dream after it, give a complete picture of her; and we may notice that
here, as wherever she is excited and kindled out
of her dull misery, her qualities of intellect come
out, and her language is of extraordinary richness
and beauty. Notice too with what a firm subtle
touch it is brought out here that it is Odysseus
that she cares for most; she has just been saying
that her anxiety is greater for her son than for
"that other," but as soon as the phantom says it
is sent by Athena, she at once turns her inquiry
to him, with a new passion of eagerness. It is
an index of her loneliness that her sister's appearance even in a dream unlocks the frozen fountains
of her heart. It is the first lifting of the darkness.

This astonishingly beautiful scene, with its
subtle psychology and its thrilling emotion, is the
noble close to the prelude of the *Odyssey*, Books
I.-IV. Penelope does not reappear till Book XVI.;
but she is kept in the picture meanwhile by repeated
references; in the scene of Calypso's uneasy taunt
(Book V.) and Odysseus' adroit and dignified
answer (Odysseus is never at a loss how to deal

with women—Nausicaa, Arete, Circe, Calypso,
Penelope herself except once): in the strange
pathos of the speech of Anticleia's ghost (Book XI.)
that begins and ends on her; καὶ λίην κείνη γε,
"surely and over-surely she abides and awaits
you," and "mark this" (the pageant of dead Queens
which was to pass before him), "that you may tell
it to your wife hereafter": and perpetually in the
expressed or implied contrast between her and her
cousin Clytemnestra which is a recurring keynote
from the beginning of the poem to the end.

The return to her is led up to, with incomparable skill, in the passage describing Telemachus'
thoughts during his sleepless night at Lacedaemon,
put (according to the epic formula) in the shape of
counsel given by Athena.

> Take heed now therefore lest against your will
> She bear away your substance, knowing still
> What kind of heart is in a woman's breast,
> That ever she is fain his house to fill
>
> Who weds her : and the children whom she bore,·
> And him who was her wedded lord before,
> From her remembrance, after he is dead,
> She blots, nor asks about them any more.

Towards the end of Book XVI. the scene shifts
back to the palace of Ithaca.  Penelope reappears;
she reproaches Antinous bitterly with the plot to
kill Telemachus.  He is taken aback and speech-
less, but Eurymachus, always ready with his quite
unconvincing falsehoods, makes a glib reply:
"There is no danger for him while I am alive; I
will protect him at the risk of my own life."  She
is too miserable to make any answer, but goes
away and cries herself asleep.  She is very near
breaking point.

Early next morning Telemachus returns; and
her welcome, weeping and clinging to him and
kissing him, has no trace of jealousy or reproach.
But he is rather short with her: "Do not break
me down," he says. "The word took not wing
from her"; she goes silently away. But later in
the day, when he comes in again with Theoclymenus to give 'him dinner, she is spinning by the
doorway and makes a touching appeal to him;
then at last he tells her the story of his voyage,
still with reluctance, hurriedly, and constrainedly.
There is a wonderful touch here. "Nestor," he
tells her, "sent me on to Lacedaemon to Menelaus:
there I saw Argive Helen." Not a word more
about her; he keeps back Helen's fondness for him
("darling child" she had called him); and her gift
of the embroidered gown "for your wife to wear
on her wedding day; till then let your mother keep
it for you in her chamber." Penelope would hardly
have welcomed this trust. Herself she makes no
reference to Helen, either here or elsewhere. The
constraint between mother and son has come back.
All the comfort she gets at this interview is from
Theoclymenus.

Later on the same day Odysseus himself comes,
and slinks into the hall in his beggar's disguise;
Antinous throws a footstool at him, which shocks
even the suitors. Penelope hears the tumult; she
sends for Eumaeus into her bower and tells him
to bring the beggar to her: she has just seen him
through the doorway, and even that unrecognising
glimpse has moved her strangely; she actually
laughs, the only time she does so. When Eumaeus
brings back word that the stranger thinks it wiser
not to have his interview till night has fallen and

the suitors have left, she answers quite contentedly:
"He seems to be no fool, whoever he may be."
From this point on, to the *Niptra*, the dramatic
tension of the story increases and centres about
Penelope.

In Book XVIII. (after the episode of Irus) she
speaks to Eurynome. "My heart moves me, as
never heretofore, to show myself among the
suitors." This was "the counsel of Athena to
make her more precious than before to her husband
and her son." It was what we should call an
unconscious cerebration. Eurynome, who is no
witch, advises her to wash and anoint herself first:
adding that "it is no use weeping for ever, especially now when you have such a fine grown son."
This was not the kind of comfort Penelope wanted:
she answers a little testily, "Do not talk like that;
the gods have made my beauty fade." Then Athena
casts sleep upon her and increases her beauty in
it: when she awakes, it is as a new woman. The
suitors' "knees are loosened with desire of her."
For the first time in the poem she speaks to
Telemachus firmly and with authority, "When you
were a child you had more sense than now"; and
he, for the first and last time, answers humbly and
deprecatingly. The splendour of her beauty moves
Eurymachus to compliment her: "You excel all
women in loveliness and stature and inner wisdom."
In her answer to him there is a new accent of
strength, and then she goes on to taunt the suitors
with meanness and tell them to show their love by
gifts. "Odysseus was glad, because she enchanted
them with soft words, but her mind purposed
otherwise." He read her like a book.

Now comes a great scene. Night has fallen:

Odysseus and Telemachus have removed the
armour, Telemachus has gone to bed in his own
room across the court, and Odysseus is left alone.
Then Penelope comes back into the fire-lit hall.
Her women clear away the supper, and go.
Odysseus and Penelope are alone, with the old
nurse Eurycleia in the background. She asks him
who he is.

Odysseus begins by fencing with her and paying her magnificent compliments, as to a strange
queen. This sort of thing generally made her
shrink up into herself; now it unlocks her; she
positively chatters to him, pouring her soul out
to him as she had never done to any one; she tells
him all about herself; they sit talking for hours.
With a pretty touch of coquetry she says at last
that it is time to go to bed. " How shall you know,
guest, that I excel other women in wisdom, if you
are not bathed and clad well in my house ? " The
ice about her heart is unfrozen :

> —This embalms and spices
> To the April-day again.

During the feet-washing Penelope sits in a sort
of dream, and notices nothing. Then he draws up
to her again and she comes to herself, and breaks
out in the most marvellous of all her speeches,
with the incomparable nightingale-passage in
which the lyric note at its highest and purest is
caught and merged in the epic structure. She can
hold nothing back from this stranger : and ends by
telling him how she means to set the contest of
the axe-heads. She can hardly tear herself away,
but at last goes. Odysseus cannot get to sleep for
a long time. When he does at last, Penelope is

just awaking from a dream of him.  Her exaltation
of the night before has faded away from her in the
grey light of the morning, but has still left her
highly strung: her prayer to Artemis, beginning:

> Goddess and mistress, fain were I that thou
> Wouldst pierce my bosom with thine arrow now
> And take my life from out me, Artemis,
> Daughter of Zeus, to whom in prayer I bow:

> Or that a whirlwind from the earth might tear
> And hurl me forth upon the ways of air,
> To fling me where the backward-flowing tide
> Of the Ocean-River leaves the seabanks bare:

> Even as the daughters born to Pandarus
> Of old were taken by the whirlwinds thus,
> Whose parents by the gods were slain, and they
> Left orphans in the palace perilous,

is ineffable in its beauty: this, and the nightingale
speech, are her high-water mark, and almost, if
not quite, the high-water mark of the *Odyssey*.

As always, her thoughts and heart are all with
Odysseus; she says nothing of Telemachus.  And
he on his side is incurable.  That same morning
he asks Eurycleia whether the stranger has been
properly treated: "My mother for all her wisdom
is a desperate one for treating an inferior man
with distinguished courtesy and sending a noble
one away without honour."  He does not know
that Eurycleia knows.  She does not undeceive
him; her answer begins with a dignified rebuke.
"Do not lay blame where no blame is to be laid,"
she says, and then she adroitly launches on a long
account of the supper and bed that Odysseus had.
She silences him thus, and then turns to her work,
bidding the maids bestir to prepare the hall: "the
suitors will be here early, for this is their high day."

There follows a long episode or series of episodes, making a prelude of calculated delay before the climax, and ending with the insulting conduct of the suitor Ctesippus and the terrible second-sight of Theoclymenus : and, just at the end of Book XX., we are told Penelope was sitting opposite and heard it all. After dinner (Book XXI. now), she brings out the bow : there is a touch of tenderness almost passing into weakness, when she sits with it on her knee in the treasure-chamber, crying for a long time : then she recovers herself, goes into the hall and carries out the action that she had so carefully rehearsed ; her speech to the suitors is almost verbally repeated from what she had said to Odysseus the night before. In Telemachus' taunting speech to the suitors there is still a little edge of temper against Penelope : " The prize is a wife such as there is not in the Achaean land : you know it ; why should I praise my mother ? Yet, if I could perform the feat, she might leave the house with any of you and I should not grieve much."

She stands by the doorway while the suitors one after another try to string the bow, and fail. Odysseus asks to be allowed to try, and Antinous rates him. Then Penelope for once asserts herself and intervenes. Eurymachus, as before, takes up the word and apologises. But Telemachus, also strung up to high tension, turns on her almost angrily : " I am master here, and give or refuse the bow to whom I please ; go away." It is more than she can stand : she goes away silently, and becomes again the Penelope of Book I., crying herself to sleep.

She sleeps all through the slaying of that awful

afternoon.  When it is over, Odysseus calls Eurycleia, but does not allow her to awake Penelope until the bodies have been removed and the hall purified.  Then she goes up with her news. Penelope thinks she has gone mad at first: and when she repeats, with detail, the incredible story, still will not believe: "Some god has done this; it is difficult to fathom the devices of the immortals."  She descends, to see for herself.

By this time it is almost dark.  She sits down opposite Odysseus in the firelight, but keeping a long way off, against the wall, and stares at him where he sits by one of the pillars round the hearth.  Neither speaks.  It is more than Telemachus can bear.  Μῆτερ ἐμὴ δύσμητερ, he breaks out, "ever your heart is harder than stone."  She answers quite gently: "My child, if it is he, we shall know each other."  Odysseus smiles: "Let your mother try me: soon she will know better." But still she stares silently; till at last even he, for the only time in the whole *Odyssey*, seems to lose control of the situation; he angrily bids Eurycleia prepare a separate bed for him.   Then Penelope's chance is come; she tells her to bring out the bed 'from the bridal-chamber.  For once Odysseus is outdone at his own craft, and gives her the sign she has been waiting for.  It has come at last, the full assurance; she bursts into tears, rushes to him and flings her arms round him.

This is the end of the *Odyssey* according to the ablest Alexandrian critics; and  certainly  the remaining 624 lines are in a different key, and look like the work of a continuator, for whom the story had come to mean more than the epic treatment, handling perhaps, as Professor Bury thinks, a draft-sketch left unfinished at the poet's death. Yet even here there are two or three fine touches; her making no reply to her husband's directions to keep still indoors and ask no questions when he leaves her in the morning: Laertes' lament that she had not mourned over him and closed his eyes: and the eager question of Dolius when Odysseus has made himself known, "does wise Penelope know you are come, or shall we send to inform her?" "She knows already," is the answer; "no need to concern yourself about that." The single line sounds almost unfeeling; really it is the brief expression of complete and triumphant confidence.

In this Epilogue to the *Odyssey*—for such in any case it is, whether it be the work of the same poet or not—the central point is the scene of the "Second Nekyia." It is very splendid, but it does not belong to the main structure and is almost "out of the picture." It can only be got in by ignoring what is an apparent absurdity, that the ghosts of Achilles and Agamemnon are supposed to be meeting and conversing for the first time, though they had had opportunity of doing so for nine years or more. It is of course devised, and devised with high dramatic skill, to lead up to a final and emphatic reaffirmation of the contrast between Penelope the good, and Clytemnestra the evil wife. The narrative of the slain suitor Amphimedon, summarising the story of the whole poem, is followed by the formal and explicit contrast placed in Agamemnon's mouth between the two women, and the memorials they leave to mankind for ever:

Thereat the son of Atreus' ghost begun
And said : O fortunate Laertes' son
Odysseus many-counselled, who a wife
So virtuous and excellent have won !

How rightly minded from of old was she,
Icarius' child, unblamed Penelope !
How well remembered she her wedded lord
Odysseus ! therefore undecayed shall be

Her fame for worth, among mankind so long
Shall the immortals make a lovely song
Of chaste Penelope, not like to her,
Tyndareus' child, who plotted deeds of wrong,

Slaying her wedded lord ; with loathing fraught
Shall be her lay upon the earth, who brought
Ill fame on the whole sex of womankind,
Even on such as righteousness have wrought.

It is the moral of the *Odyssey*, and is given
almost expressly as such. But an epic poem
transcends this way of looking at a story; it has
not a moral; or if it has, it does not state it
formally. The dramatic contrast has been
emphasised from the beginning, and kept before
us throughout by repeated touches. Though the
force and splendour of this passage are admirable,
yet the *Odyssey*, as a poem, does not need it. A
moral is a comment on a poem ; it is no part of
the poem itself.

What I have tried to put before you is the
poetical evolution of a wonderful figure under
the handling of a great poet. The initial *motif* is
given by the contrast between the two cousins.
This develops into the studied portraiture of a
perfect wife. And the perfect wife is a term of
large extent. It covers, for instance, in Shakespeare, both Imogen and Lady Macbeth. But

further, the Homeric Penelope is a special type. The contrast, expressed and implicit, is not merely of the two cousins, but of the three. For the Helen of the *Odyssey* is also a perfect wife, though she had not been so always. It is not only Menelaus who finds her so ; readers of the *Odyssey* who are perfectly frank with themselves would not have a moment's hesitation in choosing whether they had rather have known Helen in Lacedaemon or Penelope in Ithaca. So secure is a great artist of his work, that he can afford to let the heroine of his story be outshone, even in a sense eclipsed, by a figure who is secondary in the construction. Helen speaks kindly and affectionately of her cousin ; Penelope cannot even bear to let Helen's name pass her lips.[1] Penelope has all the virtues, except perhaps—dare we say ?— magnanimity ; but Helen has what is more potent than virtue, that magical, overpowering charm which has made the generations of mankind, from the elders of Troy downwards, in love with her. The crowning triumph of the poet of the *Odyssey* is that he has got both, constructionally and vitally, upon his canvas; and as regards Penelope, that under his vivifying imagination, Penelope herself has become flesh and blood. In his subtle, loving, understanding delineation, with its delicate humour and restrained pathos, she has ceased to be a special type, and become an individual, a living woman, with her nobilities and her weaknesses ; like one of Shakespeare's women.

There is an instinctive and inevitable tendency

---

[1] The passage, XXIII. 218–224, which would make an exception to this statement, was recognised by Aristarchus as an interpolation.

F

to wonder how the story went on, and to try to
fill it up in imagination; the more so, the more
that one appreciates the vivid reality of Penelope's
figure. A poem ends, but life does not. "Which
of us is happy in this world? which of us has his
desire, or having it, is satisfied?" How did she
bear the coming on of age? Did death come to
her also, as it was to come to her husband, "very
peacefully," far away from the sea? Poetry is
more real than history; but is its reality, after all,
only a strange illusion? It is part of this illusion
that one can hardly help feeling and regretting, as
in actual life, the misfits in families. Helen understood Telemachus in a way that makes one sure
that she would have been a perfect mother to a
son of her own; but she had none. And if
Penelope had only had a daughter, it would have
made all the difference to her. Even now, after so
many centuries, she makes us try to get beyond the
picture, as though it went on behind the frame, or
if we looked at it long enough and steadily enough,
would step out of the frame on to the floor. So
difficult is it to realise that, out of the *Odyssey*, the
Penelope of the *Odyssey* does not exist at all.

This is the power of art, and beyond all, of
poetry.

> He will watch from dawn to gloom
> The lake-reflected sun illume
> The yellow bees in the ivy bloom,
> Nor heed nor see what things they be,
> But from these create he can
> Forms more real than living man.

But the instinctive desire to look behind the
frame is one from which the artist himself is not
always exempt. In the Epilogue to *War and*

*Peace,* Tolstoi (that great artist who hated and despised art) wrenches, as it were, a corner of the frame back; he shows us the lovely, brilliant, and passionate Natasha Rostov become, a few years later, a commonplace middle-aged woman, dully absorbed in her husband and children, exacting, tiresome, and unreasonably jealous. Tolstoi might (he certainly did, here and elsewhere) do as he chose. But the author of the *Odyssey* also did as he chose, and we had better be grateful for his choice and leave it so:

—Be it as it was,
Life touching lips with immortality.

## V

## THE ALLIANCE OF LATIN AND ENGLISH STUDIES

An Address to Joint Meetings of the Branches of the Classical and English Associations at Oxford, Liverpool, and Leeds in January and February, 1923.

It is the first aim of the Classical Association to promote the well-being of classical studies in this country, and to secure their recognition and effective pursuit as an element in the national civilisation. Second only to that aim, and so intimately connected with it as to be really another side or aspect of the same thing, is another; to enforce the organic unity of these studies with the whole sphere of humane letters, and the unity of that sphere itself with others, with those of the physical sciences, of social and economic studies, and of the creative or interpretative arts.

The unity of education, now becoming more and more realised as the key to problems and the solution of conflicting claims, is the converse of the unity of life, individual and national. It is a unity which exists and should be recognised, as one may say, in three dimensions, not as only linear or superficial. Education should be continuous, from the elementary school to the university. It

76

should not be confined to any social class. It should be an initiation into the whole world of human knowledge or human activity.

This was an ideal which was once, for the time being, translated into fact; or so at least it was believed. In the Middle Ages the universe was strictly limited, both in time and in space; so were its contents; and so likewise was the total sum of knowledge. In the thirteenth century a *Summa Theologiae* was actually produced by a single mind. That, no doubt, was the achievement of specialisation, of the concentration on scholastic philosophy which had narrowed down and even to a large degree crowded out the larger humanism of the twelfth century. But a *Summa Anthropologiae* was theoretically at least, then and long after, conceived of as equally possible. Even in the early seventeenth century, before the prodigious expansion of science which was about to take place, Bacon could speak of taking all knowledge for his province.

Can that ideal be restored? Can humanism in the fullest sense of the word be reinstated, with a new and a larger meaning? That is the question which lies at the basis of the whole theory and practice of education. In an age of increasing specialisation, at a time given over to the pursuit of short-cuts and the invention of substitutes, when the weight of accumulated knowledge, already greater than can be borne, is multiplying almost daily, can we recover that grasp of the unity of learning which is at once the symbol and the substantiation of a sense of the unity of life? If so, it is clear that the first thing to be done is to discard bodily the idea of competition of studies,

and replace it by the idea of their co-operation
and mutual reinforcement.

The antagonism between the so-called humanistic and the so-called scientific studies in the field
of education, which a generation ago was so acute,
is rapidly becoming a thing of the past.  Common
ground was arrived at six years ago, with an
agreement which removed the fundamental principle involved from the sphere of controversy.
It is stated in the resolutions then unanimously
adopted by the Joint Conference of the Council
for Humanistic Studies and the Board of Scientific
Societies.  In effect, that concordat defined education as a single thing: that is to say, as the
training of intelligence and character which befits
the citizens of a free and civilised nation, concerned
with the thoughts and acts of mankind as recorded
in literature and history, and with the laws and
processes of nature as ascertained and applied by
science.  By a long circuit, and after many diva-
gations, we find ourselves returning to the old
doctrine, but with an enlarged scope and fuller
content.  The Seven Liberal Arts were the legacy
of the ancient world to the Middle Ages.  That
title was popularised, and brought into universal
currency, by Martianus Capella about A.D. 500.
Their content was the sum and substance of the
whole of secular culture as it was then understood; and it included, in the *trivium* and *quadri-
vium* into which it was divided, the full sphere of
humanistic and scientific studies.

So far, so good.  But the spirit of competitive
antagonism has shifted its ground, and sprung
up, in some quarters with almost equal violence,

within the field of humanistic studies themselves.
Among matters of controversy at the present
day we may note (they are far, of course, from
exhausting the list) the conflict between the professional representatives of ancient and modern
languages; the claim put forward, not without
attractive plausibility, on behalf of geography
(which is both a scientific and a humanistic
subject) as covering in its largest sense nearly
the whole field of education; and the still more
widely urged claim for English studies as giving
complete humanism, or at least all the humanism
that is attainable or required.

These subjects are dealt with at large, and pursued into much detail, in the *Reports* of the three
Government Committees on Classics, English,
and Modern Languages. I may assume in this
audience a general knowledge of these *Reports*,
even where they have not been thoroughly
mastered or subjected to detailed analysis. Even
a superficial acquaintance with them is sufficient
to show that, starting from different points, they
reach different conclusions. Perhaps they can,
largely at all events, be brought into harmony.
But it would be idle to say that they do not
require to be brought into harmony, or that they
do not here and there, either expressly or by
implication, take sharply conflicting views. The
particularist or competitive view is specially to
be noted in the attitude taken up in the Modern
Language Committee's *Report* towards Latin.
More than once it is spoken of as though it were
the enemy. "Latin should not be compulsory in
any part of a Public School" (§ 122). "It may be
hoped to rid schools of the burden of compulsory

Latin" (§ 124). "Latin should not be allowed to imperil the success of French" (§ 132). The words "burden" and "compulsory" are both invidious, and meant to raise, or to confirm, a prejudice. It would lead to clearer thinking if for "burden" were substituted "discipline," and for "compulsory," "essential." The implication in the phrases actually used in the *Report* is that in an organised system of education, Latin either (1) does not matter one way or the other, or (2) is something, like the piano, that it is to be regarded as an extra, not as an organic element. But the last of the three sentences quoted contains a fallacy still more dangerous; for it rests on a fundamental misconception of the object of education. That object is, as is sometimes forgotten, to educate. "The success of French" is to be measured by the degree to which the time and effort spent on it have helped towards developing, training, mobilising for active exercise, the latent capacities of the whole nature, intellectual and moral. You only imperil success, in its real sense, by looking to some immediate by-product. The object to be kept in view is not the success of French, or for that matter, the success of Latin, but the success of education.

Between English and Latin also there has been raised a certain amount of this artificial and unfortunate competition. It has been mainly raised in the field of university studies; but, here as elsewhere, universities and secondary schools are organic members of the body of higher education. The controversy has been conducted in the main with good temper on both sides; but it is serious enough to make it very necessary to

examine the matter, and to see whether, in the
interest not of Latin nor of English but of education as a whole, of national culture and large
citizenship, the conflicting doctrines may not
coalesce in a larger synthesis.

In such an inquiry, we may neglect the
extremists on both sides. There are still a few
reactionaries who think—or at least who say—
that to Latin as the staple of humane education
all that needs to be added is Greek. And there
are some enthusiasts for English studies who say
—or at least who think—that the Latin influence
has only been an alien and disturbing element in
the English language and literature; that *Beowulf*
is more important, both for linguistic and for
literary study, than *Paradise Lost*, and (as I have
heard it boldly put) that English, as a subject of
serious study, came to an end in the fourteenth
century. But the whole body of rational opinion
is, I think, converging on the view that Latin and
English studies are complementary; that they
reinforce and vitalise one another in the most
powerful way; and that, as their union in history
created the language which we use and the literature from which we draw our spiritual sustenance,
so their union in education supplies, for the
individual and for the nation, the core of humanism.

For an education consisting of nothing but
Latin and Greek there is neither justification nor
excuse. But (except possibly in a few highly
conservative preparatory schools : so, whether
rightly or wrongly, it is alleged) such an education
does not exist. On the other hand, past neglect
of the mother-tongue and of our native literature
in English education excuses, although it does

not justify, the excessive claims made for this study as all-inclusive and self-sufficing. Once more it must be repeated: what we have to look to is not the interest of a subject, be that subject what it may. It is the interest of the human beings concerned, as individuals and as a community; it is the development of their powers and capacities, of their understanding of life and their control over it: it is their mental and spiritual enfranchisement. As regards secondary schools, this position hardly requires defence. But a university likewise, while its students will all to a greater or a less degree specialise in their course of studies, does not exist for the purpose of breeding specialists. It has, or ought to have, a larger function; that of nurturing and sending out into the world, equipped and trained, the best type of citizens, citizens of their own country and of the world. It can only keep itself free from the sterilising effects of a narrow specialisation, by keeping prominent, in theory and in practice, the unity of knowledge, the interdependence and co-ordination of studies.

This is why it is so important that Associations formed to promote different branches of study should keep in close touch with one another, and why joint meetings of the local branches of two or more such Associations are of such high value, both as a symbol of common aims and interests besides those specially attaching to each, and as helping towards mutual understanding and harmonised action through the discussions—even, it may be, through the minor controversies—which they carry on. And this is so very specially and very obviously in the province of the two branches of humanistic study which we are considering to-day.

Let me then here cite some apposite sentences from the *Reports* of the Prime Minister's Committees on Classics and on English, to show how nearly, in this matter, they speak with one voice; how strongly the correlation and interdependence of Latin and English studies impressed itself on both Committees in the result of their investigations and of the evidence submitted to them.

"We regard Latin as of great and almost irreplaceable value as a means of promoting the proper use of the English language, both in speech and writing, by all classes of the community."

"All our experts recognise that Latin provides an incomparable discipline for modern linguistic studies." [1]

"A knowledge of Latin civilisation is indispensable for the full understanding of the languages, law and society of a great part of Europe, including the British isles."

"We see in the classics sources of our own language, our own art, our own experience, and we hold that no student of English will have completed his exploration or gained all its advantages, until he has ascended the stream of literature and discovered these perennial sources for himself." [2]

Noting, then, these theoretic conclusions, and attaching to them the weight which they deserve, yet not proposing them to ourselves or to others for blind acceptance, let us turn from them to facts.

---

[1] *Classics Committee's Report*, pp. 11 and 17.
[2] *English Committee's Report*, paragraphs 8 and 12.

The correlation or interfusion of Latin and English studies is, as an aim consciously and deliberately pursued in our educational system, a thing of comparatively recent growth. So far as it has gone, it has been of great value to both; and there appears no reason to doubt that, as it develops further, its value to both may be greatly increased.

The most obvious benefit of the conjunction has been to Latin. Latin had, through artificial isolation, and intensive study too early and too exclusively pursued in the textual and grammatical field, become partly sterilised or atrophied. There was some ground for calling it a dead language. I may note here in passing, that the same danger exists for English. It too is capable of being made a dead language. "It would be a grave misfortune," as the English Committee's *Report* (paragraph 7) justly points out, "if a defect of method which has proved injurious in Latin and Greek were to appear also in the teaching of English literature"; and co-ordination of the two studies helps largely to secure that the defect shall be avoided in both alike.

But now, we may say of Latin (1) that the scientific study of language as an operative function and a live organism has brought it about that there is no such thing as a dead language; all languages being actual live embodiments of language, and Latin being such an embodiment of peculiarly intense vitality; (2) that the same holds good of the scientific study of literature, all literature (and Latin literature eminently so) being the live expression of human thought, imagination, emotion, and experience; and (3) that under this quickening impulse Latin language and literature are now studied not abstractly as a gymnastic, like a sort of mathematics—though that abstract or technical study is not without its educational value, and a rational claim may be made for it as an intellectual exercise and a stringent mental drill—but as keys, or rather perhaps we might say windows, admitting to the spectacle and lesson of human history, of what mankind at its highest has thought and felt and done, and to the mechanism through which human thought, feeling, and action are most perfectly expressed or recorded.

But the benefit of the conjunction is no less important to English studies; and this is becoming better realised, though the conjunction itself is not yet fully accepted, still less is fully attained. The introduction of new studies into a long-established system is never quite a simple thing; it involves some disturbance of habits, some risk of friction and misunderstanding. Schools or faculties of English in the universities were initiated under difficulties. Excessive claims of enthusiasts clashed with the passive, if not the active, opposition of conservatism. It was urged that a school of English was a soft option; that it meant dilettantism and "chatter about Harriet." In order to counter that charge, artificial bones, as one might call them, were rather awkwardly inserted into the scheme of study. Moeso-Gothic was included in the linguistic study of English, though the Italic dialects are not regarded as a necessary part of the study of Latin. And more largely, the tendency was to treat English, both the language and the literature, as Teutonic, and divide it sharply from the languages and literature of the Latin nations, and from the Latin which was their common source.

It is true that English is a native product, an insular growth, with a continuous history of its own. But of that history the Latin influence is an essential part. The noble Icelandic prose of the eleventh and twelfth centuries was insular in the full sense; it derived nothing from Rome; it was outside of the European movement, to which in turn it contributed, until quite recent times, nothing whatever. England, though not exactly in Europe, was never disconnected from Europe. For nearly a thousand years the connection has been close and fertile. European prose, as a fine art, is a Latin creation; it is the prose of Cicero, the vehicle which the Roman genius gave to the world. The structure of organised and fully civilised English prose is essentially Latin. The Latin influence in our poetry is still more patent: "the descent of poetry," in Gray's well-known words, "is from Greece to Italy and from Italy to England." "Italy" in that sentence includes both the earlier and the later product of the Latin genius, both Latin and Italian poetry. Virgil is the culmination of the former and the inspiring source of the latter.

It is worth remarking here, that what has tended to make Latin and English studies drift apart is our loss of touch with Italian literature. Dante and Boccaccio were the creators, it might almost be said, of modern poetry and prose, including our own from Chaucer downwards. It is needless to mention as sources Petrarch for the English lyric, Ariosto for Spenser, Tasso and

Guarini for the whole of English poetry of the seventeenth century. But all those writers were the inheritors and recoverers of the Latin tradition. Both in prose and in poetry, of course, the Latin influence reached us very largely through France; and for this as well as for other reasons, knowledge and study of French is essential towards any scholarly study of English; this, however, is so obviously true and so fully recognised as hardly to need mention.

But the point on which I wish to lay particular stress is apart from any indirect transmission; it is the enormous importance of the direct Latin influence. Cicero and Virgil I have already named. Quintilian is a live force, not only for the arts of literary composition and criticism, but for the whole theory and practice of education. Livy and Tacitus are masters and models for historians. Ovid has been, even more powerfully, the master and model in narrative poetry from Chaucer onwards. Horace, perpetually imitated and perpetually inimitable, is almost, one might say, an English poet. Seneca and Plautus are more important than the Attic dramatists in the historical evolution of the English drama. There is no need to labour the point that alike for the linguistic and the literary study of English, Latin is essential, whether we have regard to grasp of organised syntax, to the laws of structural composition, or to appreciation of artistic form. Nor was it ever more essential than it is now, when English studies are menaced by a new peril, not that of particularism and over-specialisation, but that of diversion to merely vocational or commercial purposes. It is a safeguard against the tendency to convert schools

of English into schools of journalism. With a
school of journalism as such we need have no
quarrel. It is what it purports to be. But it is a
technical or vocational training, not a course of
humanistic and liberal education.

There is, however, another point, often ignored
or slurred over, in which the conjunction of Latin
with English studies bears directly and vitally on
English literature in both its aspects, as regards
appreciation and as regards production, as an art
studied and an art practised. That is the reference
of literature to a standard.

It is acknowledged that our own literature,
while immensely rich, is chaotic; that it is, and
always has been, to some extent undisciplined.
Structure, logic, clarity are not its strong points.
The national tendency, in this as in other respects,
has been to muddle along and to muddle through.
And conversely, we up to the present have never
had, or never had at least since the Middle Ages,
any system of national education, or any thought-
out co-ordination of the whole field of human
studies. Our culture—including science as well
as letters—has, like our empire, grown up casually,
more or less at random, in a habit (not a fit) of
absence of mind. Successive fields have been
attached to it, if one should not rather say dumped
upon it, finding a place where they could, sometimes displacing or cramping others for no
particular reason. Each, so far as it has aimed at a
standard at all, has had to form a standard for itself,
slowly and imperfectly. The examination incubus
itself has perhaps been to some extent a disguised
blessing, inasmuch as it involved a serious effort
to secure some sort of equivalence both in amount

and even, so far as practicable, in quality, of the work required to qualify for degrees or other symbols of proficiency.

The absence in our civilisation of any English Academy was noted long ago not indeed as a cause, but as a collateral sign, of the lack among us of a standard for English as for modern humanistic studies generally. It is likewise an old remark, that the tradition of classical education in our universities and public schools did in fact, to a considerable degree, supply that want. In this contention there was a good deal of truth. But the particular point I would emphasise here is this : that while even for the study of English as a matter of pure linguistic the discipline and tradition of Latin are of high value, for the English language as a vehicle of thought and an instrument for use, and for English literature throughout, Latin sets a standard as nothing else does, not even Greek. For long it did so quite consciously. It set up, as a goal to be kept in view and more and more nearly reached by continued effort, classic quality; and in particular, the Latin qualities of precision, gravity, dignity. English literature was formed and moulded through centuries of assiduous study of Latin, and through constant translation from Latin, in both the senses of the word "translation." Translation (or transference) of quality took effect through the exercise of the habit and art of translation in its more limited and more customary sense.

In this last we may trace stages of progress and changes of aim, theoretically distinct though in practice they overlap and intermingle and combine, and though no one of them has ever existed free

G

from intermixture with the others.  From Bede and Alfred onwards, translation from Latin into English was practised towards what may be called the making of English; the making it, that is to say, into a competent instrument, a practicable vehicle, of consecutive thought and organised expression.  Later, though still at what is from our point of view an early period, translations assumed their chief importance as a means of getting at what was called, in a compendious phrase which has not even now lost its meaning, "the wisdom of the ancients," of making the secrets of knowledge accessible.  Later still, we come to the great age of translations from the Latin, the seventeenth and earlier eighteenth centuries, when the object became more and more to fix and heighten a standard for English, and thus, as well as by other means, to get English fully incorporated with the Republic of Letters.  This aim is very clearly brought out in the collateral practice (often carelessly dismissed as an eccentricity or a folly) of translating English original works into Latin. The Latin versions, to name a few outstanding instances, made in the seventeenth century of *Troilus and Criseyde*, of the *Faithful Shepherdess*, of the *Paradise Lost*, were not mere idle pedantry. They had a real meaning, namely, to bring English literature under the test of a classical standard. And conversely, the innumerable translations from Latin into English, while they often had other objects as well, were meant to establish that standard, as one to be aimed after and attained, whatever else might be added to it, in original English writing.

The many phases through which the practice

of translation from Latin has passed, the varied
uses which it has served, should make us alert
to realise that the usefulness of translations themselves is very limited. The results come from
the art or exercise of translating, not from the
translations, which are transitory products. I
mention this, though it is sufficiently obvious, in
order to point out the fallacy in the popular
doctrine that the value of Latin—or for that
matter, of Greek—can be got out of translations.
A translation, like a photograph of a painting, or
the piano-score of an orchestral symphony, can
give much, though not perhaps, even at its best,
so much as these. It does not give, it does not
even pretend to give, the thing itself. This is true
for ordinary appreciation, but doubly true for
advanced study.

In other quarters again, the divorce of Latin
and English studies is defended by an argument
which involves a subtler, and therefore perhaps a
more dangerous fallacy. "We do not believe,"
says the *Report* of the English Committee, "that
those who have not studied the classics or any
foreign literature must fail to win from their native
English a full measure of culture and humane
training." Curiously, this sentence comes within
a few lines of the other sentence in that *Report*
which I have already quoted: "We see in the
classics sources of our own language, our own art,
our own experience, and we hold that no student
of English will have completed his exploration or
gained all its advantages until he has ascended the
stream of literature and discovered these perennial
sources for himself." The two statements seem
not quite consistent: and if in view of this we

examine the former carefully, we shall find that it contains more than one ambiguity. It is not clear whether by "must fail" we are to understand "do in fact fail." It is not clear whether by "a full measure of culture" is meant anything more than "a large measure of culture"—which of course no one would think of denying. But these are perhaps rather of the nature of debating points, and not really material. The substantial ambiguity is in the words "native English." What is our native English? It consists of a language and literature saturated with Latin, moulded into their actual shape by continuous Latin influence. Neither scientifically, nor historically, nor culturally is English a thing self-contained and isolable. The study of English, in each and all of these three aspects, requires for its effective conduct immediate direct knowledge of Latin as an influencing force, an organic element. For its advanced study, that knowledge must be not only direct, but wide and accurate. Linguistically it was the Latin language itself, culturally it was the Latin classics themselves, that were the motive force, the organic factor, in national development.

And conversely; study of Latin that is not to risk landing itself in pedantry and sterility, or at least to be narrowed into a mere intellectual exercise, requires, from the first and throughout, to be organically connected with the study of English. Knowledge is needed of the links and fibres which connect Latin vitally with our own language and thought, our own history and civilisation. It is not merely that there are daily lessons to be learned from Roman history, from the aims and methods, the achievements and failures of Rome. There is a still greater gain, to get into vital contact with the Roman mind and temper. Pure or abstract scholarship is an ideal, if it be one,—and I should be the last to undervalue it—only for a few exceptional people. To be largely useful, it must be embodied; it must be brought into contact with actual speech and thought and with what they express: even more than that, with what they create. For language is, in one form or another, the motive force towards all action, and towards all production. Classical scholars have somehow fallen short, have missed something of what scholarship can give, if it has not given them a standard in accuracy of thinking, in capacity of expressing, in faculty of persuading; and if they have not translated that standard into practice, in the conduct of life and the exercise of citizenship.

The claim for co-ordination, or even in a sense for fusion, of English and Latin studies, for their organic unity in the sphere of liberal education, is inherent, if we think of it, in the very name of the classics. The classics, in the proper sense of the term, are not anything written in Latin or Greek; they are what, in these or other languages, has been best written, so written as to create and fix a standard. They are peaks that signal to one another. Their standard is that of perfection; some kind of perfection, to fall short of which, in that kind, is not to be a classic. The mistake used to be made of thinking not merely that all the kinds of perfection that mattered were those, and nothing more than those, which were exemplified in the writings of ancient Latin and Greek authors: but further, that these

were not exemplified elsewhere.  And, as one
mistake leads to another, it came to be assumed,
in a confused sort of way, that anything written
in what had come to be called the classical
languages, in Greek or Latin, was a classic in
virtue of that fact.  That attitude led straight off
into classicism.  Insistence on the value of the
classical standard is not a plea for classicism.
Goethe, in well-known and highly provocative
words, said, " The classic is health, the romantic
disease."  Classicism is also a disease ; or if we
dislike that word, we may call it a "culture" in
the pathological sense of that term, which infects
the constitution and growth of literature.  The
coalition of English and Latin studies is one of
the surest safeguards against the evils of classicism, as well as against the greater evil, lowering
of standard or even loss of any sense of standard
at all.  If we smile at Goethe's dictum, we ought
to remember that when he uttered it, there were,
broadly speaking, no German classics ; German
literature was a welter, partly because it had
never gone to school to Rome.  In English, there
are the classics of romanticism.

The history of the terms " the classics " and
"classical," and of the fluctuations in their meaning
is itself a study of much interest and of no little
intricacy, and one which incidentally is extremely
instructive.  " The classics," in the ordinary
current usage, is a term of comparatively modern
origin.  As early as 1607, "the classical authors "
is found, apparently, not quite certainly, meaning
Latin and Greek authors.  The usage, however,
did not become established until a century later.
Addison's celebrated phrase of "classic ground "

in his *Letter from Italy* wavers between the two senses. The earliest citation of "the classics" in its modern meaning given in the *New English Dictionary* is dated 1711. In the sixth century A.D. *classicus* meant "a student" in the general sense, and the studies it connoted were those included in the circle of the seven liberal arts; but throughout the Middle Ages, Latin (there was no Greek) was usually spoken of as *grammatica*, "grammar." At the revival of learning many phrases came into use for what we call classical studies, no one of them with exclusive authority or even marked predominance over others: *humanitatis studia, vetus eruditio, bonae literae, optima studia, literae humaniores*. This last, the favourite phrase but not, I think, the invention of Erasmus, still survives at Oxford, though now with an altered content; and in some at least of the Scottish Universities, the older title of the Chair of Humanity is not quite displaced by that of the Professorship of Latin. In the Founder's Statutes for Magdalen College, Oxford (1458), the subjects of study prescribed, other than theological, are the *artes humanitatis*. It was in respect of these that the Degree in Arts was given. There are degrees now, as there are university courses, of many kinds and many names; but that a degree in Arts should be given to students who have never qualified in Latin at any stage and who may never, whether at school or college, have learned any Latin at all, is a thing which we may reasonably regret where it exists, and justifiably oppose where it is suggested.

The modern contraction or specialisation of usage is perhaps unfortunate, though it has its

conveniences.  But there is this much in it (to set
Greek aside for the moment, and think only, as
we are now doing, of Latin), that Latin *as a whole*,
over a period of something like six hundred years,
has certain really classical qualities, characteristic
of it throughout, only fully realised in the real
classics, but imparting themselves to some degree
to inferior or un-classic work as well : in particular,
a wonderful weight and precision.  This may be
estimated both by trying to turn pieces of what
we would call good average English into Latin,
and by trying to express the same substantial
thought in both languages, and noting how slack
the texture of the English as compared with that
of the Latin is under that test.  This is, in fact, one
important lesson to be learned—there are others
as well—from the practice of what is called, oddly,
composition ; the turning of given English, that is
to say, into Latin.  This is sometimes fancied to
be a mere trick, and a waste of time.  But, if
properly handled, it is an exercise of which there
is more likely to be too little than too much.  It
is of extraordinary value towards forming a habit
of precise thinking.  I speak of prose, not verse
composition : the making of verses in our own or
any other language we are trying to master is also
a valuable exercise in management of words to
the best advantage, and in appreciation of words
so managed ; but that is rather a different thing.

The main point, however, to which I would
return from this digression is, that the Latin
language, and the literature in which Latin most
fully realised itself, are not only large sources of
our own language and literature ; are not only
germinal forces still working in English as they

have done for a thousand years ; but give, in
important matters, a fixed, high, and permanent
standard of what may be called perfection, of a
quality, that is to say, which is perfectly satisfying,
and beyond which nothing else has gone or can
be imagined as going. English studies must still
be pursued with this standard kept in view.
Without this coalescence and interpenetration of
studies, it can hardly be hoped to get full appreciation of what constitutes, in our own mother-tongue
or elsewhere, classical quality in the true sense
of the term : still less to look for that quality, to
require it, to attain it in the actual use of language,
spoken and written ; that is as much as to say, in
the conduct of life on a fully civilised plane.

The standard is best held in view if we keep
returning for it to a separate body of literature,
and to a language which though not our own, is,
or may become, for us almost a second mother-
tongue.   It can be elicited, no doubt, out of the
enormous mass of English literature itself; but
only with much difficulty, the mass is so great
and the mixture in it so great likewise.   Also,
such of it as belongs to our own day and fills our
foreground is too close to us to make it easy
to abstract qualities from it and appraise them
at their true value.   The bulk of every one's
English reading, and the whole of one's English
writing, is necessarily of this kind ; and by far
the greater part of the English now being
written and read is, to use the old and expres-
sive phrase, "in the vulgar tongue." It has not
what, six hundred years ago, Dante re-created
and named, the *bello stile*.

Dante knew quite well that he was re-creating

poetry. He says so, in so many words, in the
*Purgatorio: Qui la morta poesì risurga.* Human
language has, in fact, never been used with greater
elevation and splendour. Yet to him it was
doubtful whether any language but Latin (he did
not know Greek) was good enough for the greatest
literature whether in prose or verse. Latin alone
was *perpetuo e non corruttibile*, alone was *sovrano e
per nobiltà e per virtù e per bellezza.*

When Dante wrote thus, he was himself a
classic, and was creating modern literature. He
could not foresee its developments. But he realised,
as we shall still do well to realise, how long a way
there was to go before the *bello stile* of Latin could
be reached in other languages. *Componimento in
stile mezzano* is his paraphrase of the name *Com-
media* which he gave to his own poem. The
growth of the forest since then could not have
taken place—at all events, it did not—but for its
drawing nutriment continuously from the ancient
soil. Language and literature are one thing, as
history is one evolution. They are the vehicle,
the manifestation, the record of the spirit of man.
That is what is meant by humanism.

In what I have put before you, I have purposely
dealt with the *media axiomata* of the subject, not
with particular methods of putting them into
application. In what ways, by what devices,
English and Latin studies can be co-ordinated to
the best effect, here or elsewhere, in schools
and in universities, is matter for careful discus-
sion among experts and practising teachers or
organisers. The considerations I have urged are
preliminary. Discussions may be largely futile

if they do not start from some concordat, from a common ground of accepted fundamental principles. For their conduct, joint meetings of those who represent more particularly the interests of cognate studies—and all studies are cognate—are of great value, and I hope they may become habitual. Particularism of studies is a perpetual danger. But to overcome it is not beyond the wit of man. It is largely due, so every one agrees, to the pressure of the examination system. There is no need to enlarge on this : the disease has been diagnosed often enough : the problem of its cure has yet to be solved. But the cure will not be effected by tinkering with machinery : all parties concerned must have, from their different points of approach, a common aim in view, the consolidation of humanism, the re-instatement of the commonwealth of studies. It will be sufficient for the moment if I have convinced you, or rather have strengthened your conviction, that close vital contact of Latin and English studies is for the advantage of both, and what is still more important, for the advantage of a large, liberal, deeply rooted humanism, pursued on scientific method, and remote alike from shallow dilettantism and narrow pedantry.

# VI

## VIRGIL'S ITALY

THE object of this sketch, so far as it goes beyond the immediate scope suggested by the title, is to emphasise, and to illustrate on a few of its many sides, the new insight into the classics, and in particular into the works of the Greek and Roman poets, given by historical, geographical, and archaeological studies. The armament of scholarship collected during the last generation by indefatigable, minute, and as sometimes it may seem even trifling or futile research, has become a constructive, or if any one prefers to say so, a reconstructive power. The ancient world—ancient and yet intimately akin to our own, which grew out of it—is becoming every year more real. No less marked is the growth in our intelligent appreciation of those classics for the sake of which classical studies are in the last resort pursued. Read with this added insight and in this new spirit, they are more than works of art, though it is as works of art that they have their primary and inexhaustible value. Our comprehension of the ancient world and its civilisation, increased as it has been and continues to be both in quantity and in quality, and also transfigured by a new power of discerning its motive forces and coordinating the details of its records, is making the classics more real, more solid and vivid. This is so with poetry as well as with history; and in poetry, nowhere with more illumination and fruitfulness than in the greatest of the Latin poets. Virgil is the voice of his age, of his race, of a whole civilisation; but very specially he is, for all time and all peoples, the poet of Italy. The sketch which follows offers suggestions towards his study in this view by considering first, what Italy was in Virgil's time and what it meant to Virgil; and secondly, what his poems, in conjunction with the ascertained facts of his life and with collateral evidence, tell with regard to his knowledge of Italy and his unique power of interpreting that knowledge in the terms of poetry.

The idea of Italy—one of such influence on human life for the last two thousand years—is in a sense Virgil's creation: at least he gave it substance, he made it part of world-thought, and contributed very largely to launch it on history. The epithet of *Romanus*, which became attached to his name soon after his own lifetime, partly obscures this. For while he was the poet of Rome, the interpreter of the Roman character and destiny, his Rome was in the largest and fullest sense Italian. The keynote of the *Aeneid* is to be found less in the initial statement of his theme,

Tantae molis erat Romanam condere gentem,

than in the final acquiescence of Juno—that is to say, of all opposing ideals and thwarting influences —in the will of Fate at the end of the poem,

Sit Romana potens Itala virtute propago.

This unifying note had already been clearly

CARL A. RUDISILL LIBRARY
LENOIR RHYNE COLLEGE

sounded by him in the *Georgics*, where the phrase
(ii. 176) *Romana per oppida* comes as the final
touch in the *Laudes Italiae* and proclaims the whole
of Italy Roman, and Rome herself Italian.

Even as a geographical expression, Italy had
only just then taken its full meaning.  In earlier
times the peninsula, marked off though it is from
other countries by unusually obvious boundaries,
possessed none but a merely physico-geographi-
cal unity.  It had been the meeting-place and the
battle ground of many races, languages, civilisations.  The Latin League, pivoted on Rome, was
in perpetual conflict with the hardy and warlike
nations of the interior, Volscians and Marsians
and Pelignians.  North of it was the once great
Etruscan Confederacy, reaching from the Po
Valley down to Rome itself and the "Tuscan
Tiber."  Beyond it were the wealthy and powerful
Celtic tribes of the Cisalpina, and the Ligurians,
a separate race who offered an obstinate resistance
to assimilation.  On the south was the great
Samnite League, which had overrun and absorbed
by sheer weight of pressure the Greek cities of
Campania; and beyond that, wide regions divided
between native Apulians or Bruttians and the
numerous colonies of the Greater Greece.

Italy as a political term begins to exist with
the organisation of 197 B.C., after the Hannibalic
War, when it was put under the consuls as distinct from the four transmarine provinces then
created.  This was followed by half a century of
hard fighting north and south, which gradually
began to weld Italy into one.  A policy of intermixture of races was deliberately pursued.  In
180 B.C. nearly 50,000 Ligurians were transferred

bodily to Samnium. At the same time, the network of Roman colonies, connected by military
roads, was continually drawn closer, both in the
north and in the south, by fresh foundations.
This process of artificial fusion has its limits and
its perils. Its use on a larger scale under the
Empire was one of the solvents of the Imperial
fabric; for it cut at the roots of provincial patriotism. But here the immediate result was twofold;
for while on the one hand it weakened the resistance of tribal or local units to assimilation, on the
other hand it developed among them a common
resentment against Roman interference, and out of
this arose some imperfect feeling towards Italian
unity, and a sense of Italian nationality.

The clash between the two movements, the
absorption of Italy by Rome and the rejection of
Rome by Italy, was inevitable. In 125 B.C. the
Fulvian rogation, *de civitate sociis Italicis danda*,
opened a struggle which went on for fifty years.
It culminated in the Social or Italic War of 91 B.C.
This broke out in consequence of the triumph of
the reactionary party in Rome, the repeal of the
*leges Liviae*, and the murder of the great statesman
who had passed them. Rome then missed her
mission; the allies were the unitary party. Their
new capital at Corfinium received the name of
Italica. The centre of gravity of the peninsula,
it should be noted, was not yet moving north-
ward, as it did later, beyond the Apennines; for
the Lombard Plain was in effect a foreign
country.

The revolt was broken, partly by fighting,
mainly by concessions. In 89 B.C., a Roman Italy,
now extending as far as the Po, was in some

sense recognised; though, seven years later, the Samnite march on Rome was only arrested by the battle of the Colline Gate, and, later still, fragments of the Confederacy were still in arms, unsubdued and unreconciled.

Virgil was born just after the desolating Servile War, which followed directly on the destruction and disorganisation wrought by the Social War, had been stamped out. The long struggle, accompanied as it was by frightful civil bloodshed, massacre, and proscription, had left Italy a wreck. But its unification had in effect been won. When Virgil was twenty-one, the citizenship was given by Julius Caesar to the country between the Po and the Alps. A few years before he began to write the *Georgics*, the whole of the Cisalpina was formally incorporated with Italy. Rome and Italy had coalesced. There was a body, but it was drained of blood. The embers, in the phrase of Horace, were still hot.

Both the old constitution of Rome and the prosperity of Italy had gone to wreck. The influx of material wealth from the transmarine provinces seemed likely to be as disastrous in its effects on Italy as that from the Indies was, many centuries later, to Spain. Italy was bankrupt, was half-depopulated; much of its vast potential wealth was derelict. For the task of reconstruction, the first requisite was peace. That was secured by the Empire. But the next, and one of equally vital importance, was a new creative impulse, a new ideal. The question was, could a united Roman Italy be established ideally and actually? Could it get rid of the evil legacy of the past, while retaining or renewing the stimulus

of its ennobling traditions? Could it be got to
prosper, to believe in itself and its mission, to
hope, to work, to be contented?

It was Virgil, more than any other—artist or
historian, statesman or administrator—who supplied the spiritual force for the new Italy. His
vision of Italy was also a creation. He is the
first and the greatest of national Italian poets.
For any full realisation of his genius and appreciation of his art we have to study—and we
cannot study with too much or too minute care—
the living picture he presents in his poems, first,
of the land itself, its detailed natural features, its
unequalled beauty; then of its nationalities and
their heroic and historic past, its kinships and its
place in the world; and, lastly, of the tasks, the
hopes, the ideals which he sets forth as the interpreter of the new order and the newly created
nation.

The facts of his life which are relevant are
both simple and well known. He was born and
brought up near Mantua; was educated at Cremona
and then at Milan; studied, read, and wrote for a
good many years at Rome; then lived chiefly in
Campania, on the coast and inland, and also, in
his later years at least, much in the *secessus Italiae*,
the less frequented and no less beautiful interior
of Central Italy. Apart from his native Mantua
and his chosen Parthenope, there are but few
direct references in the poems to places personally
known by him; the *memini vidisse* (*Georg*. iv. 125)
of the old Cilician's garden outside Tarentum is
almost if not quite unique, and the *monstrantur*
in his description of the Valley of Amsanctus
(*Aen*. vii. 563) only suggests, without expressly

H

affirming, an actual visit of his own. But internal evidence crowds on us of a knowledge both wide and intimate of many districts throughout Italy from the Alps down to the Straits.

The importance of his Mantuan birth and up-bringing has been exaggerated among those who have sought to trace specifically Mantuan land-scape all through the Eclogues and even in his later poetry, though, as we shall see, it has been undervalued or forgotten in another way. His landscape is, in fact, seldom Mantuan except where expressly named as such. But more largely, he does not allow us to forget that he is a North-Italian, a Lombard, as Dante calls him. He was a student at the University of Milan in the most susceptible years of youth ; and we may readily believe that it was in vacation rambles and *villeggiature* that he gained the wide personal know-ledge of Lombardo-Venetia and the Tyrol shown in the poems. The ancient, like the modern, Milanese flocked up into the hills in summer. Virgil's excursions must have ranged not only over the Adige and Po Valleys,

> liquentia flumina circum
> Sive Padi ripis Athesim seu propter amoenum,[1]

but in the alpine and sub-alpine hill-country, from Monte Viso, *pinifer Vesulus*,[2] in the west right across to the country which sixteen centuries later was Titian's, and whose colour and atmosphere the Mantuan poet has rendered with as intimate truth as the Venetian painter. He speaks of the great lakes, Como and Garda,

> lacus tantos, te Lari maxume teque
> Fluctibus et fremitu assurgens Benace marino,[3]

---

[1] *Aen.* ix. 680.  [2] *Ib.* x. 708.  [3] *Georg.* ii. 159–160.

with an accent of personal passion.  He has been
with the herdsmen while they gathered medicinal
herbs in the mown sub-alpine pastures, where
the Mella winds its way through the hills by
Brescia, *tonsis in vallibus et curva prope flumina
Mellae.*[1]  He has followed the coast round the
Venetian Gulf to the sources of the Timavus—the
repeated allusions to this in *Eclogues, Georgics,*
and *Aeneid*[2] point to some special intimacy—and
far up from it into the Tyrolese highlands with
their castellated dolomitic rocks, *aerias Alpes et
Norica castella in tumulis,* where the aurochs still
roamed in virgin forest (*Georg.* ii. 374;  iii. 532)
and the clear streams " purer than amber " gushed
down into the plain.   Twice over in the *Georgics*[3]
he draws a vivid picture of the north-eastern
coast of Italy from Ancona upwards, describing
with intimate precision the waves of the Adriatic
racing to shore before the east wind, and the same
scene in a more violent Etesian gale (the modern
Bora) that comes down from the mountains of
Friuli over the "floating fields," driving the long
rollers crowded before it and ruffling up the deep
cornfields of the land.

> Qualis Hyperboreis Aquilo cum densus ab oris
> Incubuit Scythiaeque hiemes atque arida differt
> Nubila : tum segetes altae campique natantes
> Lenibus horrescunt flabris summaeque sonorem
> Dant silvae longique urgent ad litora fluctus.

Most of these passages are in the *Georgics ;*
and it is there that Virgil's North-Italian patriotism

---

[1] *Georg.* iv. 278.
[2] *Ecl.* viii. 6 ; *Georg.* iii. 475 ; *Aen.* i. 242-249.
[3] *Georg.* ii. 107-108 ; iii. 196-201.

shows itself most strongly. When we pass to the *Aeneid*, Northern Italy recedes more or less into the background, and the Southern-Central area takes the prominent place. But the *Georgics* themselves were written in Campania, on the Bay of Naples, and in the exquisite hill-country inland; and the colour of their landscape is very largely Campanian. It is particularly to be noticed how much the sea and the seashore enter into his picture of agriculture. A dozen instances will at once occur, but one or two may be specially noticed. The *nigra harena*, the dark volcanic sand cast up by the ground-swell (iii. 240–241), is, as Sir Archibald Geikie has pointed out, the peculiarity of that coast, and unknown either in the Adriatic or the Upper Tyrrhene Sea. The shell-gravel recommended (ii. 348) for orchards and vineyards, which Virgil did not find in the orginal agricultural treatise which he is at this point following, but is, so far as we know, an insertion of his own, implies close proximity to the coast, for otherwise the labour and cost of haulage would have been prohibitive. This applies also to the reference (iv. 47–48) to the use of calcined sea-shells as a fertiliser.

The Central Italy of the *Aeneid*, covering not only Latium and the hill-country behind it, but the whole region now known as the Abruzzi, together with Umbria and Etruria to the north and Campania to the south, is described, and intimate knowledge of it shown, by a hundred illuminative and suggestive touches. These are crowded in the Catalogues of Books VII., VIII., and X., but the whole of the last six books are full of them. Take one instance to serve for many, the group of names in three closely packed and enriched lines (vii. 682–684):

> Quique altum Praeneste viri quique arva Gabinae
> Iunonis gelidumque Anienem et roscida rivis
> Hernica saxa colunt, quos dives Anagnia pascit.

The extraordinary skill of the epithets is no less wonderful than the exquisite music of the language. They are as vividly descriptive now as they were then; Palestrina high on its hill, glittering across the wide rolling Campagna; Castiglione down in the plain, with its highly cultivated monastery-lands, inheritors of the domain of the Gabine Juno and its fragments of decayed greatness; the rushing Teverone going from its cold mountain-springs past Subiaco to its leap into the lowland by the falls of Tivoli; the People of the Rocks (that is what the name Hernici means in the old Marsian language) among mountains still described in modern guide-books as "everywhere watered with beautiful streams and clothed with magnificent woods of oak and chestnut"; their capital, Anagni, in the fertile lower country, filled with temples and sanctuaries, which retained its riches and its holy places through the Middle Ages and was the favourite country residence of the Popes.

Here, as elsewhere in a hundred places, Virgil's epithets, descriptive phrases, collocations of names and words, are an endless field for appreciative study which can hardly be too minute. Personal knowledge here is of course far the best; but much is to be got from books of travel or description, and not a little from photographs like those, for instance, in Cervesato's *Roman Campagna*.

We may note here in particular a few of the
epithets, lumps of distilled and crystallised
romance of which Virgil alone had the secret:
*turrigerae Antemnae,* the town (like San Gimignano)
*delle belle torri; frigida Nursia,* five thousand feet
up in the thin, clear air of the Apennines; *olivi-
ferae Mutuscae,* where the old name is lost but the
epithet survives in the modern village of Oliveto;
*maliferae moenia Abellae,* the grey walls gleaming
through apple orchards in a combe of the Campanian hills; the *vitrea unda* of Lake Fucinus, the
great sheet of clear, pale water in a basin of lime-
stone hills, drained now and intensively cultivated,
but within living memory still "a far-spreading
mirror for mountain and sky." [1]

New light is often thrown by acquaintance with
Italy on passages which by being carelessly read
lose half their beauty and most of their significance.    Instances are, the *Fescenninas acies aequos-
que Faliscos* (vii. 695), the sharp-ridged hills
springing out of the flat Tiber valley; the landscape in vii. 800–802:

> viridi gaudens Feronia luco
> Qua Saturae iacet atra palus gelidusque per imas
> Quaerit iter valles atque in mare conditur Ufens,

with its picture of the wooded hill with its gushing
springs rising out of the sombre marshes by
Terracina through which the Ufente makes its
way slowly and laboriously towards the sea; and
very remarkably in the noble simile (xii. 701–703):

> Quantus Athos aut quantus Eryx aut ipse coruscis
> Cum fremit ilicibus quantus, gaudetque nivali
> Vertice se attollens pater Appenninus ad auras.

[1] *Aen.* vii. 631, 711, 717, 740, 759.

The relevance of the simile has been challenged, on the ground that while Athos and Eryx are detached, towering masses rising abruptly out of the sea and the plain, the Apennines are a long mountain range. But Virgil is not speaking of the Apennine range, he is speaking of *pater Appenninus,* "the lord of Apennine." If we look for this, it is clear enough; it is the central peak, now known as the Gran Sasso d'Italia, which, rising to the height of ten thousand feet, and visible from both Adriatic and Tyrrhene seas, dominates the landscape and keeps its snow-clad summit right through the summer into July. But that is not all; seen from the south across the Mid-Italian plateau, the helmet-shaped peak gives the vivid effect of a gigantic warrior striding along the ridge.

The more carefully we study Virgil, the more we shall realise that when describing Italy or any part of Italy he is everywhere true to nature, though he wraps it all in his medium of strange gold. It is worth noticing by contrast that his Carthaginian landscapes, coast and inland, so far as not conventional, are merely those of Italy copied, and his Mount Atlas is like an Alpine mountain range, with pine-clad peaks and rivers fed from snowfields or glaciers.[1]

So much may be said, by way of introduction and as suggestions for a closer study, about Virgil's Italy from the point of view of the lover of the country, the landscape artist, the picturesque geographer. But equally important and fertile is his interpretation of its economic condition and the economic movement of the time, in relation

[1] *Aen.* iv. 248-251.

particularly to agriculture and national products, but also to commerce and industry. Here we are immensely helped by Varro.

How great the debt of Virgil to Varro was, not only in this matter but throughout, we cannot know unless and until Varro's own lost works should be recovered, but may guess from the constant use he makes in the *Georgics* of the extant treatise *de Re Rustica*. There are whole chapters in that treatise which Virgil has, so to speak, taken up bodily and incorporated in the *Georgics*: "multa· ad suum hoc opus Vergilius transtulit," the phrase of the Servian commentary, is less than the truth. Good instances may be studied in *R. R.* I. xxxix., the whole of which is full of phrases taken over in the *Georgics*: it is worth special remark how the *nonne vides* which Virgil took from Lucretius[1] occurs, as good current prose, in the "nonne videmus" of Varro; and in *R. R.* II. ii. 9–11, a passage the main substance of which may be quoted:

Haec magis ad villaticos greges animadvertenda. contra illae in saltibus quae pascuntur et a tectis absunt longe portant secum crates aut retia, quibus cohortes in solitudine faciant, ceteraque utensilia. longe enim et late in diversis locis pasci solent, ut multa milia absint saepe hibernae pastiones ab aestivis . . . eaeque ibi, ubi pascuntur in eadem regione, tamen temporibus distinguntur, aestate quod cum prima luce exeunt pastum, propterea quod tunc herba roscida meridianam quae est aridior iucunditate praestat. sole exorto potum propellunt, ut redintegrantes rursus ad pastum alacriores faciant, circiter meridianos aestus, dum defervescant, sub umbriferas rupes et arbores

[1] *Georg.* i. 56.

patulas subigunt, quaad refrigeratur, aere vesper-
tino rursus pascunt ad solis occasum . . . ab occasu
parvo intervallo interposito ad bibendum adpellunt
et rursus pascunt, quaad contenebravit: iterum
enim tum iucunditas in herba redintegrabit. haec a
vergiliarum exortu ad aequinoctium autumnale
maxime observant.

Here the last two paragraphs are transferred
bodily, but with added poetical loveliness, to
*Georg.* iii. 322–338, while the first paragraph gives
the immediate suggestion for the lines (339–345)
in which Virgil continues, though he applies the
material to a different setting.

These and other passages Virgil has distilled
and transfigured: they have become poetry under
his hands; but like all poetry, they remain a record
and interpretation of actual life. The modern
commentator on the *Georgics* will stick by Varro
and the other writers on Italian agriculture and
economics, and will, by comparison, neglect the
Greek literary models, Aratus or Nicander.

The publication of the *de Re Rustica* in 37 B.C.
synchronised with the inception of the *Georgics*.
An object of both works was to promote the
economic reorganisation of Italy, in which agriculture was the staple industry, by turning the
revived taste for country life among the educated
and wealthy classes to practical use. Something
of the same kind is being attempted in England
now; and here as elsewhere archaeological and
historical research has results of more than a
merely abstract value. One striking feature in
the *Georgics* is the way in which the doctrine of
small holdings, the watchword of "back to the
land," exists side by side with the capitalisation

in large masses of agricultural wealth. The precept of "exiguum colito" is advanced on mixed grounds, economic, political, and sentimental; yet simultaneously a contradictory ideal is unconsciously dominant, that of "latis otia fundis," the pleasantness of those *latifundia* which were too much for the small holdings in the end.[1]

But the matter in Virgil's mind, or at least in the mind of the statesmen who inspired him, was more than agricultural reorganisation; it was the creation of new wealth by a fuller exploitation of the agricultural resources of Italy. The nation was on the verge of bankruptcy, but had enormous undeveloped wealth. The small holdings whose decay was deplored had covered only portions of the country here and there. Great parts of Italy were still virgin soil, potentially rich, but as yet unreclaimed. Much of the plains was still primeval forest, much of the hill country consisted of *calles publici*, crown lands as we should call them, let for grazing at a low value. Varro's description of Italy as one vast orchard, "arboribus consita ut tota pomarium videatur,"[2] may apply well enough to his own home in the rich country about Reate, but for the whole peninsula is clearly rhetorical hyperbole: for he tells us in the same treatise of the *mouflons*, the wild sheep that ranged over the Sabine country,[3] almost within sight of Rome, and of continuous pasturage all the way from Apulia to Reate, uninhabited but for occasional *cohortes in solitudine*, movable encampments such as those of the Libyan shepherd in the *Georgics*.[4] Virgil himself three times mentions, as

---

[1] *Georg.* ii. 413, 468.      [2] *R. R.* I. ii. 6.
[3] *R. R.* II. i. 5.      [4] *Georg.* iii. 339-345.

something quite familiar, the task of the pioneer
farmer who has to fell or burn the forests:

> silvam devexit arator,
> Et nemora evertit multos ignava per annos,
> At rudis enituit impulso vomere campus : [1]

> Ac velut, optato ventis aestate coortis,
> Dispersa immittit silvis incendia pastor,
> Correptis subito mediis extenditur una
> Horrida per latos acies Vulcania campos : [2]

and once more:

> immissi diversis partibus ignes
> Arentem in silvam,[3]

where the reference is to the systematic burning
down of forests on a large scale in the dry weather.
Draining, clearing, planting were being pressed
forward with the whole energy of the State: much
of Latium itself was still unreclaimed swamp or
thicket, just as it is represented in the later books
of the *Aeneid*. As Virgil and Horace drove with
Maecenas along the Via Appia towards Bene-
ventum, they skirted the whole length of Mount
Taburnus on their left hand. The exact year of
the journey is uncertain, but it was just when
Virgil was beginning to work on the *Georgics*.
"Iuvat olea vestire Taburnum," he writes in the
poem [4]: he had seen, then or at some other time,
those miles of southward-facing slope being
planted with olive orchards, and the sight had
been no less welcome to him than it was to the
Minister of the Interior.

The picture drawn of a returning Golden Age
in the fourth Eclogue bears close relation to the

[1] *Georg.* ii. 207-211.  [2] *Aen.* x. 405-408.
[3] *Aen.* xii. 521-522.  [4] *Georg.* ii. 38.

famous *Laudes Italiae* of the second *Georgic.* The
atmosphere, the tone and colour of the two
pictures are hardly distinguishable. Much of
what in the Eclogue is presented as the scenery
of an ideal world corresponds closely, not merely
in general feeling but in detail, to the heightened
portraiture of the actual Italian country in the
Georgic. It will be sufficient to cite half a dozen
instances where the echo is almost a literal
repetition :

> Ipsae lacte domum referent distenta capellae
> Ubera—
>
>> ipsae memores redeunt in tecta suosque
> Ducunt et gravido superant vix ubere limen.
>
>> nec magnos metuent armenta leones—
> At rabidae tigres absunt et saeva leonum
> Semina.
>
>> fallax herba veneni
> Occidet—
>
>> nec miseros fallunt aconita legentes.
>
> Occidet et serpens—
> Nec rapit immensos orbes per humum neque tanto
> Squameus in spiram tractu se colligit anguis.
>
>> nullo munuscula cultu tellus fundet—
>
>> iniussa virescunt
> Gramina.

The change is merely that the tense is altered
from future to present; as though Virgil would
say, in his silent way, " Here or nowhere is the
land and the age of gold." And the prophecy of
the Eclogue :

> Molli paulatim flavescet campus arista
> Incultisque rubens pendebit sentibus uva
> Et durae quercus sudabunt roscida mella,

similarly differs only in the angle at which it is viewed from the pictures of the restored agriculture that Virgil saw with his eyes around him:

neque illum
Flava Ceres alto nequiquam spectat Olympo ;[1]

alte
Mitis in apricis coquitur vindemia saxis :[2]

and (though a closer parallel here is Horace's *Mella cava manant ex ilice*),[3]

et apes examina condunt
Corticibusque cavis vitiosaeque ilicis alveo.[4]

A Golden Age in some distant country and conjectured future is not the matter in question, but a Golden Age which awaits us now, which offers itself for our acceptance : thought of in the Eclogue as taking shape with the growth of a child then on the point of being born, realised in the Georgics as actual.

In the Praise of Italy, Virgil no doubt carries his idealisation a good deal beyond what facts would bear out. Varro in the prologue to the *de Re Rustica* had done just the same. Both were using the recognised licence of a panegyric; it is one which hardly needs any reasoned defence, but it is interesting to note some of the points in which it may suggest prosaic criticism, if only in order to deprecate the attempts made by commentators to explain these away. *Hic ver adsiduum* [5] is evidently inconsistent with the emphasis laid elsewhere on the intense cold of the Italian winter, the *saevum gelu* of *Aen.* ix. 604,

---

[1] *Georg.* i. 95–96.      [2] *Ib.* ii. 521–522.
[3] *Epod.* xvi. 47.      [4] *Georg.* ii. 452–453.
[5] *Georg.* ii. 149.

*cum nix alta iacet, glaciem cum flumina trudunt.*[1]
The line which follows,

Bis gravidae pecudes, bis pomis utilis arbos,[2]

is only true in a few exceptional cases: swine
according to Solinus; a *bifera malus*, mentioned by
Varro (*R. R. I. 7*), as cultivated in the *ager Con-
sentinus* by the springs of the Crathis; and the
famous *biferi rosaria Paesti*.[3] The *nec miseros
fallunt aconita legentes* already quoted suggests,
if it does not convey, a false impression; for the
poisonous monkshood was common throughout
Italy then as it is now, and Dioscorides mentions
it as growing in special profusion in the uplands
of the Aternus valley. And once more:

Haec eadem argenti rivos aerisque metalla
Ostendit venis atque auro plurima fluxit,[4]

is as a statement of fact indefensible, though as a
patriotic fallacy it had a wide currency. "Metal-
lorum omnium fertilitate nullis cedit terris," says
Pliny of Italy (*N. H.* iii. 20), "in mineral wealth
of every kind it is unsurpassed in the world."
Italy is in fact very poor in minerals. It has no
silver; the Roman silver came chiefly from Spain,
or from the lead mines of Sardinia. A trifling
amount of stream-gold was found here and there
in the Cisalpina. Italian copper is small in amount
and of inferior quality; there is a little tin found in
Tuscany. But there seems to have been a popular
belief that the metals were there, and to be found
if searched for; and a recorded *senatus consultum*
forbidding mining in Italy was probably passed

---

[1] *Georg.* i. 310.          [2] *Ib.* ii. 150.
[3] *Ib.* iv. 119.          [4] *Ib.* ii. 165–166.

with the view of checking waste of expenditure
on useless borings.

In the *Aeneid*, the agricultural and economic
view of Italy naturally yields place to the larger
national and political aspect. That is a matter
which would require separate treatment. But a
few notes may be added here on the importance
given in the *Aeneid* to Etruria as representing an
older blood and civilisation, now incorporated
with and giving strength to the Latin and other
Central-Italian races more immediately connected
with Rome. The "Tyrrhene Thybris" is coupled
(*Aen.* vii. 242) with the Latin Numicus, as already
the "Tuscan Tiber" had been, in the *Georgics*, with
the "Roman Palatine." The Etruscan Mezentius
heads the list of captains in the armies of Italy.
The account of the Mantuan contingent on the
other side in the war (x. 198–206) is of great
importance. Virgil himself was very probably,
on the mother's side at least, of Etruscan blood.
In art, religion, and tradition of a distant past,
the Etrurian element in Virgil's Italy cannot be
ignored. It is significant that a Tuscan adven-
turer, *Corythi Tyrrhena ab sede profectus* (*Aen.*
vii. 209), is chosen by him, from a slender and
obscure tradition, to be named as the founder
of Troy.

This method of historico-geographical illumination may be applied interestingly to one particular
instance.

At the opening of the third *Georgic* there is a
celebrated passage which has perplexed many
readers, and on which the commentators, according to their method, do not throw much light.
After the lines in which Virgil says that the old

subjects of Greek mythology are outworn, and
that his work shall be on a new way, by which he
will bring the Muses home from their Aonian
summit, he goes on with extreme elaboration[1] to
describe a temple, a circus, and a theatre, which
he proposes to erect and embellish at Mantua,
and to adorn with elaborate sculpture in marble,
ivory, and gold, with historical statuary and allegorical frescoes.  So long as we regard this whole
description as merely fanciful, as an allegory of
his own aspirations in poetry and of the reflected
credit which they would bestow, when realised,
on his native town, the whole passage must seem
artificial, disproportioned, and not free from the
charge of being both tumid and frigid.  But when
Virgil seems to us to fail in good taste and in
fundamental constructive power, we had better
make sure that the fault lies not in his taste but
in our understanding.  It seems clear that this
passage was not so elaborated and given such
prominence without serious reason.  To understand that reason we must look to political and
administrative history.

The Peace of the Empire had not yet been
established, or the safety of Italy secured so far
as to allow of that great economic reorganisation
and development, that restoration of credit and
increase of prosperity, which was the real task of
the Government.  The menace of war in the East
still hung over the empire, but the real and
pressing danger lay, as it had lain for some years,
nearer at hand.  The Gauls were peaceful and
thriving; the tribes of Western Germany were far
distant; the troubles in Spain, though they after-

[1] *Georg.* iii. 12–39.

wards became serious, were local, and could not spread beyond the Iberian peninsula. But the storm centre was on the north-eastern frontier. Italy, as history had over and over again shown, and was to show over and over again down almost to our own time, was open on that side to invasion and conquest. In 101 B.C. the great Cimbric invasion on this frontier had forced the Consul Catulus to fall back from the line of the Adige; and the final destruction of the Cimbric horde, καθάπερ πέλαγος ἀχανὲς κινούμενον, "surging on like a vast sea," was effected by the joint armies of Marius and Catulus not far from the site of the bloody and indecisive battle of Solferino. Now, the fear to which the Italian cultivator was subject was not the distant terror of the East, "purpura regum"; it was closer and more formidable, "coniurato descendens Dacus ab Histro."[1] It was invasion on a huge scale through the Tyrol from the territories of the Austrian Empire and the Northern Balkans. Julius Caesar before his assassination had been preparing for a campaign, as serious as his earlier campaigns in Gaul, to arrest and crush the advance of the Dacians. In the confused years which followed there was imminent danger that their confederacy, united under Cotiso, would break into Italy while it was almost denuded of troops. In 35 B.C. Octavianus was obliged to make a personal campaign, in which there was hard fighting, against the restless Iapydian and Pannonian tribes on the immediate border. But nothing decisive was effected then, and meanwhile a great civil war in the East was becoming more and more threatening. For the

[1] *Georg.* ii. 497.

I

time, recourse had to be made to a policy of with-
drawal and concentration. Northern Italy lay in
grave peril: and the strategic key to Northern
Italy was Mantua.

There are two, and only two, main gateways
by which Italy can be invaded from the north-east.
One is by Laibach (Emona) and along the coastal
lowlands. The other is over the Brenner and
down the valley of the Adige. The two great
military roads leading through these gateways
met within a few miles of Mantua, probably at
Hostilia on the Po. The coast-road had been
commanded, for more than a century, by the
fortified military colony of Aquileia. The Brenner
route might be commanded by a similar position
at Verona, but the advantage of Mantua was that
it covered both. Below the junction of the Mincio
and Po, the whole country was a maze of rivers,
swamps, and canals, impassable by any large
armies, and the subsidiary coast-road from Ravenna
to Altinum was commanded in all its length by
the Roman fleet. A great fortress and garrison
at Mantua would completely block all invasion
between the foot of Lake Garda and the Po delta.
We may reasonably believe that the military
advisers of the Roman Government were pressing
to have Mantua taken in hand. Its territory had
already been settled with the disbanded veterans
of the civil war: now it might be made into a great
place of arms, the military and administrative
capital of Northern Italy.

Its military importance was no new discovery:
for it had been, as Virgil tells us, the great northern
fortress of the ancient Etruscan confederacy. Then,
indeed, it had been not merely a fortress but a

naval base. In the passage of the *Aeneid* which
I have already quoted, emphasis is laid on both
these aspects, and Virgil speaks not only of its
wealth, troops, and fortifications, but also of its
fleet.[1]

Such a project in contemplation gives the whole
passage in the *Georgics* proper setting and relevance.
But things went otherwise. The campaign of
Actium was swift and decisive; the Far Eastern
question became quiescent: and after that, the
Roman Government, when the troublesome insur-
rection in Spain had been quelled, found themselves
able to check the north-eastern peril by a renewed
forward policy. This was carried out systematically with large forces. The series of campaigns
conducted by Tiberius and Drusus in 15–9 B.C.
subjugated the Tyrol, pacified Illyricum, and drove
a wedge between the formidable tribes of Central
Germany and the Balkan kingdoms. Mantua sank
back into an insignificant provincial town. The
fleet was at Ravenna, the Pannonian legions
quartered far forward on the Drave. For the
architectural and artistic adornment which Virgil
had anticipated, Mantua had to wait until the
fifteenth century and the rule of the Gonzagas :
and when later still it became the effective military
key of Italy, it became so in Austrian hands. Once
more now the wheel has circled: Mantua is a
decayed town, its fortifications have been levelled
and its palaces are half ruinous. But Rome was
henceforth not at the centre of gravity of the new
Romanised Italy; it was not the natural capital.
When the main seat of Empire was transferred to
Constantinople, it soon ceased to be so even in

[1] *Aen.* x. 206.

name, and was replaced by Milan. How much
modern reunited Italy has lost as well as gained
by Rome becoming its capital again is a curious
question. The antinomy has always existed.
Virgil aimed at reconciling it. He partially did
so ; he perhaps did something also to perpetuate
it.

# VII

# THE VIRGILIAN UNDERWORLD

In the sixth *Aeneid* all the elements of Virgil's genius coalesce at their highest power; and in their fusion they create, so to say, a new element. Or to put it otherwise: while the whole world of Virgil's poetry is a world not merely drawn on the flat but modelled in the solid, is a three-dimensional world, and while as we search its depths and discriminate its planes in the light of increased knowledge and new methods, it becomes to us, on all the sides on which it is connected with the field of Roman studies, more and more solid, living, and fertile, in the sixth book we find ourselves, we hardly know how, transferred into a transcendental world, one of more than three dimensions. This is what gives it its mystical, here and there we might almost say its bewildering quality, and this is, in particular, what makes it difficult to relate its scenes either with geography or with history. We are moving here in a world which is imaginative in a further sense than that in which all poetry is imaginative. The agricultural subject-matter of the *Georgics*, the historical, geographical, and ethnological subject-matter of the main fabric of the *Aeneid*, are no doubt fused and in large measure transmuted by the poetic imagination: we cannot argue either from them or to them as though the

poems were prose documents.  But on matters of
fact or of history the imagination is there working
within certain definite limits which we can trace
and mark off.  Here it is working (to continue the
mathematical analogy) within limits which, so far
as the actual world is concerned, are equivalent to
absence of limit.  By ordinary criteria we do not
know, at any moment, where we are.  It is, as
will be remembered, one of the qualities of four-
dimensional space that in it an object may, so far
as the criteria of three-dimensional space are
concerned, be in two places at the same time.
This is just what we feel in the sixth *Aeneid*.  Up
to a certain point—up to line 263, to be precise—
we can follow Aeneas' movements on the map, can
place Virgil's scene, from point to point, in its
geographical and archaeological bearings.  Then
there is a faint click ; and with the " ibant obscuri "
we are suddenly in a scene of which we cannot say
whether it is real or not, nor what relation it bears
to known or ascertainable facts.

Yet in this impalpable undeterminable scene
" among the empty mansions and void realms of
Dis" (l. 269), Virgil has plunged deeper than he
does elsewhere into the recesses of what was for
him, hardly less than for us, an ancient world, half
forgotten and only recoverable in tantalising fragments, *res alta terra et caligine mersas* (l. 267) ; and
we may say with some confidence that recent
archaeological research has enabled us to understand what was in his knowledge and in his
imagination better than any one could have done
twenty years ago.  For the scene in which he sets
the drama or mystery of this book is, to a startling
degree, that of what we have now learned to call

a Minoan palace, far back in history. There is not
space here to do more than offer the most summary
sketch of what might be expanded into detail at
every point : in the notes which follow I necessarily
omit much both of fact and of inference.

Aeneas has landed at Cumae. The "Euboean
coast," the "Chalcidic fortress" (ll. 2, 17) were,
according to the current and superficial tradition,
of Greek settlement and foundation : and this, in
the artificial chronology of the ancient historians,
was fifty years later than the war of Troy. Virgil
at the very beginning of the book lays strong
.emphasis on an earlier settlement, coming from
the "Minoan realm" (l. 14) of Crete. The temple
of the sun-god on the citadel (l. 10), and the vast
underground halls somewhere below, belong to
that earlier world. On the great entrance-doors
are six panels in metal relief (ll. 20–32) with subjects
from Minoan history : the slaying of Androgeos,
the drawing of the lots, Pasiphae and the bull, the
Minotaur in the labyrinth, Theseus and the clue,
and the flight and fall of Icarus ; the last of these
panels being either missing or incomplete. This
gateway appears to be the main entrance to a vast
mass of chambers and corridors, partly at least
underground, *lati aditus centum, ostia centum* (l. 43).
In some central chamber is what may be called the
Record Office, where the utterances of the Sibyl
are "committed to leaves."[1] It is to be noted here
that the traces of pen-and-ink writing on cups of
Middle Minoan III. show that such libraries may
very well have existed, and in fact palm leaves are
conjectured to have been the substance on which
they were written. Those leaves of (shall we dare

[1] *Aen.* vi. 74 ; cf. *Aen.* iii. 443–452 for a fuller description.

to say ?) Minoan script, transcribed on rolls of linen, had for many centuries a mysterious and magical significance.

The passport for exploration of the "covered-up places of earth," *telluris operta* (l. 140), is the golden bough, which Aeneas finds in a wood somewhere between Cumae and Misenum: It was made of *brattea*, gold leaf, or rather thin gold plating, like those wreaths and masks with which we are familiar in Mycenean tombs. Somewhere in those same woods, hidden among beds of gravel, black pools of water, and thick shade of trees (l. 238), and further made difficult of access by mephitic vapours, was another entrance to mysterious underground dwellings. Here Aeneas and Deiphobe enter just before sunrise; the ground sounds hollow under their feet (l. 256), there are sounds as of dogs howling, and the treetops are shaken by blasts of subterranean wind. Then "ibant obscuri"; and we, like them, begin to move in obscurity, and find ourselves in a mysterious world.

The palaces of Dis through which Aeneas is now led, are, in their general aspect and in an astonishing number of particulars, Minoan like the palace of Knossos. Virgil recreated or imagined such a palace near Cumae, in great part ruinous, choked with rubbish or completely hidden underground: here and there waterlogged, as in that volcanic region is often the case, so that its explorer has to be ferried over a stagnant pool, the "Stygia palus" (l. 323), the "alta stagna Cocyti," thick with volcanic sand and bubbling with gases (ll. 296, 297); or moves precariously along the side of a boiling stream, Phlegethon, that issues from subterranean depths. By doorways and in corridors are sculptured figures of monsters: a couchant hound, Cerberus; a female figure grasping serpents, Tisiphone; creatures hundred-armed, three-headed, serpent-headed, beaked and clawed. The great entrance-hall is half filled by a huge elm that has grown up through the shattered pavement. The vestibule walls are covered with frescoes of allegorical figures: Grief, Sickness, Eld, Care lying on a couch, Fear, Hunger, Poverty, Violent Death, Toil, Evil Joy. Facing the entrance is a great group of War, Discord with serpent locks bound in bloody ribbons, and the Furies in iron cells. Farther on is a pool which has to be crossed in a leaky ferry-boat stained rust-red by the volcanic water (l. 303). Beyond it are more frescoed halls: one painted with the *lugentes campi*, female figures with a background of forest; another with groups of warriors. Passing through these, one comes to a great wall-space on the left built up against the cliff and painted with an elaborate representation of the city of Dis, triple-walled, and moated with a flaming torrent. The gateway of the city is flanked by massive columns and surmounted by a gateway tower plated with iron; in front of it is a seated figure of Tisiphone, wide-eyed and wrapped in a crimson cloak. Sounds are heard, as though they came from inside the walls, of blows, groans, the clash of iron and the rattle of chains. They are the sounds of volcanic action interpreted into a new meaning, the hissings and rumblings and explosions of subterranean forces. Before the scene, as it bursts upon him, Aeneas comes to a stand: "respicit subito" (l. 548);

and as he stands amazed and terrified, the Sibyl
expounds to him all the actual hell which lies
across that threshold the representation of which
is before his eyes.  Through that realm, in the
body or out of the body, she herself had been led
by Hecate when she was made priestess of the
place and received full initiation :

> me cum lucis Hecate praefecit Avernis,
> Ipsa deum poenas docuit perque omnia duxit.[1]

In that infernal world "Gnosian" Rhadamanthus
reigns and judges.; just as, in one of the portrayed
scenes past which Aeneas had already gone,
Minos the Cretan was shown holding his court of
justice and passing sentences (ll. 432-433).

After the Sibyl has finished her account, they
go forward again, through an arched gateway on
the right, and along dark corridors (ll. 631, 633) to
an entrance where Aeneas deposits his golden
bough on the threshold.  By this touch Virgil,
with his wonted subtlety, indicates that what
follows is, in some fuller sense than what has
preceded, a vision or initiation rather than an
actual journey.  No doubt what Aeneas sees
there, particularly the line of Latin heroes shown
and described by Anchises (ll. 760, ff.), from Silvius
to Marcellus, is not wholly without reference to
actual galleries of national history.  It suggests
portrait-statues, not painted panels.  Some such
gallery is probably in Virgil's mind where [2] he
describes the ancient palace of Laurentum, a
building planned like the throne-room in the
royal villa at Knossos, but also like a Roman
basilica.  In that palace also " veterum effigies ex

---

[1] *Aen.* vi. 564, 565.          [2] *Ib.* vii. 177-191.

ordine avorum astabant," carved in cedarwood,
and each figure bearing his own cognisance,
Sabinus the pruning-hook and Picus the *ancile*,
just as here, in the vision of Aeneas, Silvius leans
on his spear, Numa carries the *sacra*, and Torquatus
points towards the axe.  But the Fortunate Fields
into which Aeneas has entered, though their
scenery and equipment may be suggested by
actual places and monuments, cannot on their
large lines be imagined as corporeally existent, or
even as having an analogue in the scenes through
which he had hitherto been passing in the body.
They have an "ampler ether," "a sun and stars
of their own" (ll. 640–641).  The landscape, the
figures and actions which display themselves to
him, are visionary.  He and his guide move
through them as in a dream,

> tota passim regione vagantur
> Aeris in campis latis,

unconfined by space, unhampered by the body.
From that vision he has to return into life
through the gates of sleep.  These gates are
for exit only, not for entrance.  They are the
symbolised mechanism of the medium through
which the supernatural world projects itself
into and acts upon the world cognisable by
the senses.  Through one of them, the gate of
horn, the souls undergoing reincarnation pass
from the other world into this.  They are the
*verae umbrae*, as Virgil calls them in one of his
pregnant and many-faceted phrases; the realities
becoming shadows, or the shadows becoming
realities, according to the angle at which the
process is viewed.  Through the other, the gate

of ivory, come the *falsa insomnia*, the effluences
from another world which affect human lives as
perturbations, as unreal or perplexing dreams.
Virgil here, as usual, hints at much and says little.
A great deal of labour has been wasted on expla-
nations, more or less far-fetched, of the meaning
he wished to convey by making the spirit of
Auchises dismiss both Aeneas and the Sibyl
through the ivory gate. The primary or superficial reason is obvious : it is merely a note of
time, indicating in accordance with the current
rules of oneiromancy that the journey, begun
(l. 255) at dawn, is concluded before midnight.
As to the further meaning or meanings hinted at,
they are too delicate to be analysed.

The Minoan colour generally, and the specific
Minoan analogies, of the scenes through which
Aeneas passes between his entrance into the
cave's mouth and his deposition of the golden
bough, are obvious and need hardly be laboured
in detail : it will be sufficient to add here a few
illustrative sentences from the description of the
palace at Knossos given by Sir Arthur Evans and
Dr. Burrows. It was, they tell us, "a vast complex of chambers, courts, and corridors, hard to
find one's way through, even on the spot." "The
winding staircases and the stories piled one above
the other . . . must have made it bewildering in
the age that followed the sack, when the upper
structures were still partially standing, but
enough of them had fallen to block up doors
and passages. The very existence of basements
and upper stories would be new and confusing to
the northerner." "Whole areas were covered
with stone carvings or frescoed plaster." "On

the corridor walls were frescoes that helped out the story and suggested its details." " Everything around, the dark passages, the lifelike figures surviving from an older world, would conspire to produce a sense of the supernatural. It was haunted ground, and then, as now, phantasms were about." One is reminded of the experiences of Manolis, the Greek workman who was left as night-watchman in the Hall of the Cupbearer : how the cupbearer came alive, and the animals round began to low and neigh :

> Ecce autem primi sub lumina solis et ortus
> Sub pedibus mugire solum, et iuga coepta moveri
> Silvarum, visaeque canes ululare per umbram.[1]

" The later stories of the grisly king," says Sir Arthur Evans, " sprang as it were from the soil, and the whole site called forth a superstitious awe." The " grisly king " here is the legendary Minos ; but the phrase, as will be remembered, is Milton's used of Satan ; and in Virgil too, the palace has become the palace of the infernal monarch, the realm not of Minos but of Dis. " At Knossos," Sir Arthur Evans continues, " the tradition of the ancient sanctuary survived, and prevented the actual palace site being inhabited." " It was left severely alone by the newcomers."

What information had Virgil before him, from records or traditions or actual relics that he may have seen, for building up this picture of what looks so like a Minoan palace in the neighbourhood of Cumae ? Of some Minoan settlement there, as in other parts of Southern Italy, there was certainly some quasi-historical tradition such as is mentioned

[1] *Aen.* vi. 255-257.

by Herodotus,[1] ἀπὸ Κρητῶν γενέσθαι Ἰηπυγας Μεσσα-
πίους. The author of an interesting article on
*Symbolism in the Sixth Aeneid* in the *Classical
Review* for March, 1910, makes bold to say that
" Virgil originated the story that Daedalus founded
the temple of Apollo at Cumae," but we must take
that hardy statement in the light of another in the
same article with which we shall hardly be inclined
to agree : " the author of the sixth *Aeneid* is no
archaeologist." But that tradition so far as it has
reached us is vague and does not touch on the
*Realien* of the imported civilisation. Had Varro's
books of *Antiquitates* survived we should doubtless
have material for answering the question. As it
is, there are certain points suggested, and certain
inferences which may be drawn from them, in the
chapter on labyrinths in Pliny.[2] " Dicamus et
labyrinthos," he begins in very striking words,
"vel portentosissimum humani impendi opus, sed
non, ut existimari potest, falsum ": the sentence
might serve as a motto for an account of the
discoveries in Crete. Pliny considers the so-
called labyrinths, vast complexes of prehistoric
building, of the Graeco-Italian countries, as all
originating from or suggested by the Labyrinth
*en titre*, that in the nome of Heracleopolis on the
edge of the Fayúm in Egypt. What he says about
that labyrinth may be taken as a sort of loose but
vivid definition of what the word as applied to
other buildings means. " In it," he says (I quote
from Philemon Holland's picturesque translation),
'' are contained certain vast and stately palaces,
temples of all the gods, and a world of images and
statues, besides an infinite sort of other pieces

[1] VII. 170.          [2] *N. H.* xxxvi. 19.

portrayed in monstrous shapes . . . rooms formed in such manner that no sooner are the doors and gates opened which lead into them but a man shall hear fearful cracks of terrible thunder . . . the passages from place to place for the most part so conveyed that they be as dark as pitch, in manner of caves vaulted overhead and as dark as dungeons " ("maiore in parte transitus est per tenebras," like Virgil's *ibant obscuri per umbram*), and again, "lofts and galleries so high that he must climb stairs of ninety steps apiece ere he can land at them."

The details of the Egyptian labyrinth were matter of common knowledge in Virgil's time, and no doubt they had some share in shaping his construction. He had never, so far as we are aware, been in Egypt himself, but Gallus was his most intimate friend, and it may be assumed that during the four or five years of Gallus' prefecture many communications passed between them. Some measure of Egyptian influence may be doubtfully traced in the sights recounted by the Sibyl : they give something of the effect of a recollection of pictures seen by her as she unrolled the pages of a Book of the Dead. On the whole, however, there is little in the *mise en scène* of the sixth *Aeneid* which suggests any distinct Egyptian motive.

Pliny goes on to mention three other labyrinths : that of Crete, of which "nulla vestigia exstant": then and long before, as since then until recently, it had wholly disappeared from sight or knowledge ; one in Lemnos, of which there were a few fragments extant that he does not particularise, but as to which there seems no reason to doubt that it was a Minoan work ; and one in Etruria. This last had also wholly disappeared, but accounts

remained of it both in records and in a local
tradition which survived in Pliny's own time.  It
was also known under the name of the tomb of
Lars Porsena: it would seem to have served
among other purposes as the burial-place of the
Etruscan kings, and to have been the Westminster
Abbey, as one might say, of Etruria.  I use this
analogy deliberately, because the description of
it which Pliny quotes from Varro reads amazingly
like a distorted version of a description of some
great sanctuary, either of the type represented by
the Shwe Dagon of Rangoon with its clustered
and storied spires, or of a cathedral of the full
Gothic of our own thirteenth century, made at a
time when no architecture of that kind survived,
and when the description had thus become un-
intelligible.  One can dimly make out from it a
mass of building with flying buttresses and copper-
sheathed domes, and with a central spire or group
of spires rising from among clustered pinnacles
to an incredible height.  Varro wrote, Pliny tells
us, that he was ashamed to mention the reputed
height: according to the figures quoted by Pliny
from "Etruscan fables" it was 600 feet, exceeding,
that is, the height of old St. Paul's in London and
even of the short-lived spire of Beauvais, which
while it stood was the wonder of the world.  The
audacities of prehistoric and of mediaeval engineering were very fragile.  Beauvais collapsed twice
over.  The later of its two spires, which soared
300 feet above the gigantic roof, is described in
the account of its collapse in 1573 as a *tour
pyramidale*, exactly the phrase that Pliny uses of
the building at Clusium.  That even the ruins of
this gigantic building should have rapidly dis-

appeared is not difficult to understand when we think how little is left of the vast conventual buildings of Cluny, and how the abbey church at Westminster was only saved from total destruction by the sudden turn in the wheel of politics which sent the Protector Somerset to the scaffold.

Of the Minoan Cumae, whose existence Virgil asserts, no relics have hitherto been found. The earlier settlement was merged in or replaced by the later Hellenic city : the site and buildings of any ancient Minoan palace may even then have been avoided in superstitious awe and left to the slow decay of nature, or to the accidents of her more catastrophic action in that region of subterranean fires and insecure surface. After a long period in which it was populous and powerful, able to repel in the sixth century B.C. an organised attack by the whole force of the Etruscan and Umbrian confederacy, the Greek Cumae slowly decayed. In 420 B.C. it succumbed to the Samnite league, was stormed and sacked, and never again recovered. The New Town across the peninsula replaced it as a seaport and centre of commerce : long before Virgil's day it had sunk into decay and became the *vacuae Cumae* of Juvenal.[1] The fashionable watering-places of the earlier empire were only a few miles away; but fashion sticks close by its own resorts, and with regard to prehistoric remains the Roman business-man or pleasure-seeker, like the modern Chinese, "was not curious." We hardly hear of Cumae again until in the sixth century it resumed some passing importance as a Gothic fortress. The cave of the Sibyl, or what passed for such, was blown up by

[1] *Sat.* iii. 2.

K

the Byzantine engineers of Narses in the campaign
of A.D. 553 : and that was the end.   Since then, the
whole features of the district have changed ; new
hills have been thrown up, new lakes hollowed
out, by volcanic action; the shore along the Gulf
of Puteoli has sunk under the sea-level and risen
again ; of the great engineering works of Agrippa
near Misenum hardly a trace survives.   Possibly
there may still exist, under the modern surface,
recoverable by some daring and lucky excavator
of the future, remnants of the palace through
which Aeneas was led by the Sibyl.

# VIII

## THE ODES OF HORACE

An Address delivered to the Classical Association during the War

The Classical Association has been occupied during the rest of to-day in discussing the position of the classics in a reconstructed system of National Education. That is a subject which is of immediate and very practical importance—so far, at least, if no further, the supporters and opponents of classical study would all agree. But it is also a subject which in some of its aspects is highly technical, concerned with methods and machinery. It may be in some measure a supplement, in some measure a relief, to return from it to the classics in themselves, to what they mean for us, what we know them to be.

The great revision of values forced even on the most indolent minds by the present emergency often brings one back to old statements, which are seen with new eyes, and in which we find a new meaning. Among these is Milton's famous definition of "a complete and generous education." It is that, he says, "which fits a man to perform justly, skilfully, and magnanimously all the offices both private and public of peace and war." Few would be disposed now to reject, or even to criticise, that definition; though they might vary, perhaps, in the stress they laid on one or another part of it. Taking the word "education," not in its narrower professional sense, but as meaning the training and conduct of life throughout, I would ask you to consider for a little what is the actual value, according to the new standards after which we are feeling, of classical poetry to us, as human beings, as citizens of a great and free commonwealth, as men and women conscious individually of where our highest duty lies and resolved, at whatever cost, to do it. This is no time for intellectual any more than for material luxuries. We can only defend the study of poetry if we are rationally convinced that poetry is a function of life, and therefore a necessity if life is to be what it ought. We can only defend the study of classical poetry if we are as fully and as groundedly convinced that it is, here and now, living and life-giving; that it enables us, as individuals and as a nation, to live better, to do our duty more justly, skilfully, and magnanimously.

In such matters, it is well to avoid large generalisations. *Dolus latet in generalibus* is an old and sound maxim. I will not spend your time on theorising about the nature and function of poetry. I will take for granted, what could be shown on some other occasion, that poetry is, in all its kinds and shapes, a pattern and interpretation of life; that in its sum, in the integration towards which it is constantly moving, it is the pattern, and interprets the meaning, of life as a whole; and that the classical poets in the wide sense of that term—the poets, that is to say, who in any age or country have done what all poetry sets out to do with the nearest approach to perfection—do not so much create an imaginary world as reveal to us the rhythm, the pattern, the real truth, of the world in which we actually live.

The classical poets in the other sense of the term—the poets, that is to say, of the culminating periods of the ancient Greek and Latin civilisation—got that name because, like their great contemporaries in prose, they were felt to have set up a standard of accomplishment, and to be not merely a model for their successors but a permanent and vital possession in themselves. Among all who are concerned with classical studies, to whatever branch of these they may have particularly devoted themselves, there is full agreement as to this. But it is useful always, and more especially at a time like this, to test our beliefs, to make sure that we do not merely take them on trust and continue in them through habit; and to see whether they really mean something to us, and are such that we can not only hold them among ourselves, but communicate them to others with the life not gone out of them.

In this testing and verifying process it is more than ordinarily necessary to avoid generalities and keep closely in touch with actual instances and concrete facts. It would be easy, but it would be idle, to discourse at large about the beauty and excellence of classical poetry. In doing so, we should either be on the one hand preaching to the converted, forcing an open door, or on the other hand failing even to strengthen our own conviction, and failing still more to convince others. What may and I hope will be useful in both ways is to take up and examine a single instance; and the more we can select a crucial instance for this purpose, the better.

For more reasons than one, the *Odes* of Horace are such a crucial instance, and well adapted to the object in view. In the first place, they occupy, as having been and still being the school-book of the European world, a well-known and accepted place in any advance towards acquaintance with the classics. Secondly, they are a body of poetry which is not only historically famous, but easily accessible to all who have such educational advantages as are now widely open to all classes. Full appreciation of them is, no doubt, one of the last rewards of trained scholarship; but any one who has begun to learn Latin, and mastered its elements, can soon begin to read them, and, with or without guidance, to enjoy them and in some measure at least appreciate them. Thirdly, they are a crucial instance in this sense, that they present us with poetry stripped, so to speak, to the bone, and depending for its value on its purely poetical quality.

This last point is important. In the *Iliad* and *Odyssey*, for example, we have not only poetry, but an enthralling story, which as a mere story told in prose would be, and is, arresting and fascinating. In the Greek tragedians we have not only poetry, but the vivid representation of human action and suffering. In Lucretius we have not only poetry, but the masterly exposition of a great philosophical system and its direct application to conduct. In Virgil we have not only poetry, but all these other things as well, fused by his lonely genius into a structure which is of a richness certainly unsurpassed, probably unequalled, by any work in any language, ancient or modern. With Horace the case is quite different. The three books of *Odes* (to which for the present occasion it will be simpler to confine our attention, the fourth book being a sort of supplement) are a collection of eighty-eight short pieces—they range from eight to seventy-six lines in length, their average length being under thirty—studiously simple, deliberately restricted in range both of thought, of language, and of emotion. Many, perhaps the majority of them, seem on a first acquaintance slight and even trivial. They announce no new truths and present no superhuman ideals; they offer no unsuspected outlooks, no startling shocks of surprise. We move in them among common feelings, familiar reflections, the stuff of life as it runs from day to day. Yet for many centuries, and to countless readers, they have been not only the school-book of youth, but the handbook of mature years, the solace and chosen companion of age. Longer acquaintance only confirms and increases their strange potency. "It is only after mature experience of life that his full charm is felt, his full meaning understood": "To each successive age he seems to express its own familiar wisdom and experience." These two sentences from the pen of my own Latin teacher, William Sellar, are both strictly true; and the best supplement to them is what he adds in the same passage: "No other writer, ancient or modern, seems equally to speak to each individual as a familiar friend."

This is true throughout of Horace as a writer; but what we have to consider more closely is Horace as a poet, and the *Odes* as poetry. For this purpose comparisons with other familiar friends, with Montaigne, for instance, or Addison, are not relevant.  Poetry is a thing by itself.

It is a thing by itself in many ways ; and one of these is that it is untranslatable.  The form is the substance.  In instances that might seem to traverse this general truth, what has been more or less successfully transferred from one language into another is something bound up with the poetry—the thoughts, the incidents, the imagery, the ornament—it is not the poetry itself.  Now in the *Odes* these other things count for less than in almost any other poet.  Hence it is not surprising that, while translations of Horace without number have been (and no doubt will be) attempted, all are, in a greater or less degree, failures; they set out to perform the impossible.  Not only do they not serve to replace the *Odes* themselves ; they hardly even convey a notion of what the *Odes* are like.  And if the *Odes*, as I think they do, bear closely on life, and give a pattern of life—one, of course, among many—which is of actual and un-replaceable value to us as human beings at the present day, no further argument is needed for learning Latin enough to be able to read them, gradually to appreciate them, and to take from them into our own life what they have to give.

Let us, then, approach the point more closely, and ask what sort of pattern and interpretation of life the *Odes* offer.  It will help us to do this if we look for a moment at the circumstances of their origin, and the life of their author.

The *Odes* represent the concentrated work of Horace in poetry for about ten years, in the central portion of his life, the years in which he fully found himself. He was working concurrently on what took shape as the second book of his *Satires*. In both we see the real Horace emerging from a turbid and not very creditable youth, educating himself, creating, not for himself only, but for the world and for future times, a type of the civilised mind. He belonged by birth to the lower middle class; but, by his father's singular and self-sacrificing care, he was given the best education, at school and at the University, which the times afforded. For a good many years this care seemed to have been wasted. Reduced himself, after a short and inglorious military service in the civil wars, to quill-driving in a public office for a livelihood, he fell into bad company and very nearly went to pieces. Naturally, as he tells us himself, he was both indolent and hot-tempered; a life of dull work, tawdry pleasures, and low associates, was turning him into a sort of Dick Swiveller. The record which this stage of his life has left in the *Epodes* and the earliest *Satires* shows, mingled with the germs of finer qualities, coarseness of fibre, bad taste, vulgarity. Then, by some gift of fortune or strain of character for which we cannot be too grateful to his good genius, he got himself in hand. His early education told, it bore fruit; by the age of thirty-five he had developed that precious complex quality which the Romans called *urbanity*, a compound of good taste, good feeling, and good sense. He made himself into a man of the world in the best sense, instead of the worst, and into a gentleman. He created, it may almost be said, the type of both for the civilised world, and showed how it was attainable without high birth or wealth, without over-anxiety or ambition;

and, more than that, without either special intellectual gifts or anything that could be called
saintliness of life.  It is for this reason that he has
gone, and goes, straight to the heart of the world;
that he touches and kindles minds which are
refractory to the appeal of other, and it may be,
far greater, poets.

Part of his secret as a poet is that he knew his
own limits.  It is a weakness in him, which we see
him gradually overcoming, that he was even too
acutely conscious of them.  Only in his later
lyrics and in his *Epistles* does he become completely
free from self-consciousness, and what sometimes
jars on us a little as needless self-depreciation.
Several of the Odes let one down uncomfortably at
the end by a touch of ironical humility.  Yet even
this fault—if it be a fault, as I think we must admit
that it is—reinforces his unique power of appeal-
ing to the common mind.  We feel the exquisite
artist to be, at bottom, altogether such an one as
ourselves.  Often he seems deliberately to hold
himself back, to understate, in his dislike of
over-expression.  It is in the *Epistles*, those easy
conversational pieces which are hardly poetry at
all, not in the *Odes*, which are poetry and nothing
else, that we find, slipped in among the familiar
discourse, his most romantic touches; it is in them,
too, that we find, perhaps, his most penetrating
and mastering single phrases—two or three simple
words—"quod petis hic est"; "ire tamen restat"—
which have, for many thousands of minds through
many ages, been keys to the whole of life.

The *Odes* are the long, patient distilment of
years, during which they had, line by line and
word by word, been weighed and tested, measured

and balanced, by the most rigorous of critics, their author himself. He had his reward, and we share it: not we who are at home only, for hundreds of our soldiers have a pocket Horace as part of their field-kit, and thousands more have verses of Horace in their memories, to flash at intervals on that inward eye which is not only the bliss of solitude, but an uplifting and sustaining force in labour, weariness, and danger.

What, then, can be said briefly and truly, of the kind of poetry which the *Odes* are, of their distinctive technical quality as art, and of the pattern of life that they give?

It is a kind of poetry which does not flood and dazzle. It does not carry us into any celestial empyrean; it does not open out to us any new and luminous world. Nor is it inspired—as some poetry, but not the greatest, has been—by the passion of humanity, and sympathy for the life and labour of the people. From the great idealisms, from the intenser passions, from the deep-thrusting and far-searching range into unexplored regions, he keeps himself apart. He never touches what are called problems, whether social or individual. The sphere of poetry is co-extensive with life; that is to say, it has no limit. "La poésie," says Michelet, "s'en va cherchant aux terres lointaines. Que cherche-t-elle? L'infini." But the sphere in which Horace, by instinct and by deliberate choice, moves is quite extraordinarily limited. We have in his poetry a pattern, small, concentrated, and incredibly clear, like the reflection in a convex mirror, of such a life as all people can live, a life within the reach of the workman at his bench, or the clerk at his desk. His thought and his feeling are both, in the strict sense of the word, commonplace; but, in both, he is plumb on the centre, and his touch is certain.

It is in virtue of this centrality that the *Odes* are not merely untranslatable, but inimitable. Echoes of them, indeed, there are in all subsequent European poetry, as must needs be of a volume which has been not only the school-book but the companion through life of the European world. But rarely, and only in the hands of a few poets, has the Horatian touch been now and then recaptured. We recognise it, for instance, in the famous quatrain of Malherbe:

> Le pauvre en sa cabane où le chaume le couvre
> Est sujet à ses lois,
> Et la garde qui veille aux barrières du Louvre
> N'en défend point nos rois;

or in the pellucid cadence of Tennyson's—

> He rests content if his young music wakes
> A wish in you
> To change our dark Queen-city, all her realm
> Of sound and smoke
> For his clear heaven, and these few lanes of elm
> And whispering oak.

Our own Gray, like Horace as a fine critic and keen though detached observer of life and nature, like him in his slow, minute, and laborious production and in a wonderful power of giving a new, distinct, enduring, and arresting vitality to the commonest thoughts and feelings of mankind, is like him too in that studied felicity attributed to Horace by the exquisite phrase of a Roman critic. But none of these poets, or of others, has given to the world, as Horace has, a secular Psalter for daily and yearly and age-long use.

As with the Psalter itself, the *Odes* have in them repetitions, inequalities, faults of matter and manner. Some of their contents seem unworthy of their place : mannered, uninspired, questionable in their use and their actual present value. Some we may think (but we had better think twice and thrice) we could well do without. We have to make allowances in both for religious or literary conventions; for Jewish narrowness and vindictiveness, for Roman coarseness. But both volumes have been taken to the heart of the world, and have become part of ourselves. It is interesting to remark that both have this note of intimacy, that the Psalms and the *Odes*, or at least the most familiar among them, are habitually referred to, not by their titles (for they have none), nor by their number in the series, but simply by their opening words. We do not usually speak of the 95th or 114th, the 127th or 130th Psalms, if we wish to be understood, but of the *Venite*, the *In exitu Israel*, the *Nisi Dominus*, the *De profundis*. And so with Horace one speaks familarly of the *Integer vitae*, the *Aequam memento*, the *Eheu fugaces*, the *Otium divos*. This secular Psalter, like its religious analogue, has to be supplemented, enlarged, re-interpreted, possibly even cut, for actual use, for application to our own daily life. But both, in their enormously different ways, are central and fundamental ; permanent lights on life and aids to living.

The human value of the *Odes*, like their literary and poetical quality, may be—indeed has been—questioned. To impatient readers, as to those who ask from poetry opulence of language and sweep of imagination, they have seemed thin,

bloodless, even shallow or superficial. Their
stringently limited range of thought and feeling,
like the scrupulous frugality of their wording,
lends itself to this misinterpretation. Horace
works with a smaller palette (to use a metaphor
from the sister art) than almost any other distinguished artist : he paints almost in monochrome.
Nor is he any more opulent in design than he is
in colouring. A master of human nature, he ex-
plores no heights or depths in it : a master of
language, he employs it with unequalled parsi-
mony. He deliberately and systematically uses
for poetry the simplest and most colourless prose
words ; he makes every word, so far as possible,
fulfil a double function ; and he almost never uses
a different word or phrase where it is possible to
use the same one over again. It is simply astonishing to observe, not only how small the vocabulary
of the *Odes* is, but how there is hardly a phrase in
them which does not, with or without some slight
modification, recur. In one of his later lyrics,
where he disclaims competition with the eagles
of soaring song, he compares his own workman-
ship to that of the bee. The likeness is just : for
the effect of the *Odes* is that of the precise, delicate,
and mathematically beautiful structure of a honey-
comb, into which slowly, frugally, cell by cell, the
honey is filled.

Thus Horace's habitual under-statement or
under-expression, the way in which he limits himself to what he is perfectly sure of, makes him
able to convey it with the same certainty to the
ordinary human mind. "Ex humili potens," the
phrase which he uses himself in the Epilogue
to the *Odes*, is exactly true. It is not only that

phrases of his have grown into such universal currency that we hardly think of them as Latin—phrases like *simplex munditiis, splendide mendax, consule Planco*—but that the whole substance of what he says is of a kind to which the human mind instinctively and immediately responds. This is equally so where he is dealing with external nature and with human life; in his landscapes, each etched sharply in a few unforgettable words, whose simplicity is the translucent medium of a fine and even romantic sensitiveness, and in the ethical or reflective passages where, with an equal simplicity and an equal mastery, he fixes the lineaments of life and destiny. To illustrate this would be a task as endless as it would be delightful. Let me cite a single coupled instance in each field. Take, in the sphere of nature—and nature here means, as it always does in poetry, nature as it affects, is felt by, influences man—two winter scenes, each filling a single verse:

Vides, ut alta stet nive candidum
Soracte, nec iam sustineant onus
Silvae laborantes, geluque
Flumina constiterint acuto.

Audis, quo strepitu ianua, quo nemus
Inter pulchra satum tecta remugiat
Ventis, et positas ut glaciet nives
Puro numine Iuppiter :

and notice in them how the note struck firmly in the first word ("vides," "audis") is carried through each with the same absolute certainty: how every touch tells, and how the effect through the eye on the mind, in the first, of the still winter day after a heavy snowfall, the effect through the ear on the

mind, in the second, of the roaring night of wind
and clear frost, is kept distinct, and impressed
alike by the language and by the cadence of the
metre. "The opening," say the commentators on
the first of these two stanzas, "is copied from
Alcaeus." No doubt it is; but the point is not,
let me remind you, what a poet made his poetry
out of, but what he made it into.

Or, take again, in the sphere of reflection, of
vital interpretation, another couple of stanzas, both
dealing with that Horatian commonplace of the
transitoriness of life, the faintness of our hold on
mortal things, where he succeeds, with his most
curious felicity, *proprie communia dicere*, in giving
individual and memorable expression to thoughts
and feelings common to all human beings, and in
thus interpreting not only these thoughts and
feelings themselves, but the essential unity of all
human life :

> Cedes coëmptis saltibus et domo
> Villaque flavus quam Tiberis lavit :
> Cedes, et exstructis in altum
> Divitiis potietur heres.

> Linquenda tellus et domus et placens
> Uxor : neque harum quas colis arborum
> Te, praeter invisas cupressos,
> Ulla brevem dominum sequetur—

and note in them the grave rhythm, the ordered
arrangement, the weighed and measured words,
the parsimonious epithets. Note the two great
bell-strokes of the repeated *cedes*, *cedes*, in the
former verse; note, in the latter, the tremendous
weight of the opening word in each line, and the
setting of the three adjectives ("placens, invisas,

brevem ") trebled in their effect by their extraordinary reserve, by the fullness of meaning of all
they do not say.

Part of the secret of Horace's art is this studied
reticence, this distilment of expression into its
finest essence. It is this which enables him to
put such unsurpassed weight of meaning into
a single phrase, or often into a single word, as in
the "linquenda tellus" of the verse first cited, or
in the "morituro" and "moriture" of two famous
Odes (I. 28 ; II. 3). In this quality he gives a model
to poets, and not to poets alone, but to all of us,
which may well be taken to heart, even if it is
beyond our attainment. Tennyson, in a beautiful
sonnet, names Horace with Virgil and Catullus as
happy in having lived—

> Before the love of letters, overdone,
> Had swampt the sacred poets with themselves.

But the same applies to all speech and writing ;
they are instruments too precious to be wasted.
It was Horace who gave the counsel to poets to
keep back what they had written till the ninth
year. That counsel he gave in his own last work,
only published, as it would seem, after his death.
But he had practised it long before he preached
it. Its value is borne in on us as we regard the
torrent of poetry in particular, and of all kinds of
writing, which in these last two years has been
spouting from the press in accumulating and often
wasteful volume. Different (as different as two
things can be) in spirit and outlook, but similar in
its practical bearing, is the old counsel of the
Preacher in Jerusalem : "God is in heaven, and
thou on earth ; therefore let thy words be few."

L

It is this distilled, refined, almost monochromatic quality which shows itself in what has been called the prosaic character of the *Odes*, or of passages in them: not only in the poet's deliberate choice of the commonest and simplest words, not only in his frugal and seemingly colourless epithets, "like stones of worth that thinly placed are," but in his secure and daring use ("felicissime audax," says Quintilian) of phrases which, detached, are pure prose—"dicere quae nihil attinent," "incredibili modo consentit," "nescio quid semper abest," and a hundred others. He works in tone rather than in colour: but his mastery of tone goes along with precise and accurate drawing: in both he is one of the most searching of artists; and that is the secret, on the artistic side, of his "golden mediocrity." In that clear, colourless, and shadowless atmosphere, colour, where he uses it, tells for double.

But it is on the vital side of his poetry, on its value as an interpretation of life, that the matter finally turns; and here, too, the same criticism has often in modern times been passed on him, and the same kind of dissatisfaction felt. Life, as he interprets it to us—so this feeling may be expressed—is not only transitory, but trivial; it is an ashen-grey delight. It is in England, more than in other countries, that this feeling has prevailed; it was given wide currency by writers like Thackeray. To that view the world of the *Odes* is an old, dusty, heathen world of withered roses, guttering lights, "a cask drunk to the lees": *pulvis et umbra*, dust and a shadow. It is, in a word, the world of the dead languages.

But these languages, and the world of which

they are the recorded utterance, are, as we know, not dead but alive; and they live not only for us, but in us. The limited, bounded range of Horace's thought and feeling is central. Whatever else there may be, we must always come back to this Horatian interpretation of life as, so far as it goes, true; and added experience of life will convince us that the side of truth it gives is not only important, but indispensable. If it does not, like other poetry, lift us to the heights, it does what is from day to day as important; it leads us on the way.

A low, an unsatisfying, an unworthy ideal, is it? Well, then, let us rise beyond it. But we have no right to despise it; if we do, it is because we have failed, low as it may be, to reach it. Arnold's grave words may be recalled:

Ah, from the old world let some one answer give—
"Scorn ye this world, their tears, their inward cares?
I say unto you, see that your souls live
A deeper life than theirs."

Nor is it true that Horace's pattern of life— what is called, not very appropriately, a poet's "message"—is epicureanism, except in the sense in which the doctrine of Epicurus was one of the noblest efforts of philosophic thought applied directly towards intelligence and conduct. It goes beyond both the light sensualism of youth and the quietism, the renunciation of effort, into which that may pass later. Alongside of his "dulce est desipere in loco" stands his "dulce et decorum est pro patria mori." Alongside of his counsel to "take the gifts of the present hour," *neglegens ne qua populus laboret,* stand his great sentences of

deeply based and exalted patriotism, the "virtus
recludens immeritis mori caelum," the "Dis te
minorem quod geris, imperas "; or the succinct,
matchless portraiture of the consul Regulus,
"dissentientis condicionibus foedis," and going
quietly to torture and death for the honour of
Rome and for his own honour as a Roman. Here
is another instance of Horace's masterly reticence,
the weight of meaning given by what he does not
say. For the dishonouring terms proposed by
Carthage, as for the savagery of Carthaginian
cruelty—"inhumana crudelitas, perfidia plus quam
Punica" are words that now start to life with an
awful meaning—the Consul, as drawn by the poet,
has no abusive language, no indignant rhetoric,
no waste of precious words. *Dissensit :* "he
thought otherwise."

Yet the final word of the *Odes* is something
different from either of these; it is based neither
on the *carpe diem* of his more superficial teaching,
nor on the immortal glory of virtue. It goes
beneath these to the deepest things of all, to the
meaning of life itself for the individual soul. Here
all poetry finally meets and becomes one. No
two poets could be more unlike than Horace and
Dante. But where, at the end of his gigantic
movement through hell and earth and heaven,
Dante returns as from an infinite distance to his
final vision of the sphere of human life, "l'aiuola
che ci fa tanto feroci," "the little granary-floor that
we are so proud upon," he sees that sphere as
Horace, from his subdued, limited, but central
outlook, had seen it also. One of our own poets
has seen it too, and expressed it in our modern
language, that enriched, diluted, quivering lan-

guage which, with all its subtleties and beauties, misses the classic reserve, the classic precision, the classic imperishableness :

> In the eyes of the gods
> War-laden galleys, and armies on white roads,
> And unforgotten names, and the cold stars
> That have built all, are dust on a moth's wing :
> These are their lures, but they have set their hearts
> On tears and laughter :

not the senseless laughter and weak tears of those who live for the lust of the minute, but "the due tear," "the quiet laugh" (*debita lacrima, lentus risus*)—let me ask you to note yet once more the scrupulous felicity of Horace's weighed and measured epithets—of those who have seen life with clear eyes, known it, tested it, mastered it ; who have overcome the world.

That was what Horace had, in such measure as was within his power, done in the ten years of the composition of the *Odes*. He began the task immature, self-conscious, with a marked strain in him of coarseness and vulgarity ; when he ended it, he had wrought himself not only into a man of the world, but into a gentleman—into the Horace who fixed an attainable standard for his fellow countrymen, and for succeeding ages. He knew this himself, though it was part of the change in him that he lets that change be felt but never insists on it or displays it or preaches over it. Between the Prologue to the *Odes*, with its uncertain note, its uneasy humility, and the famous Epilogue, lies a world of self-conquest and self-realisation. In that Epilogue he has, in a few splendid lines, equally free from doubt and from arrogance, anticipated the verdict of mankind.

"I have wrought out," he says, "a memorial more
enduring than bronze, and loftier than the royal
decay of the Pyramids ; that neither corroding
rain nor furious blast may make ruinous, nor the
innumerable procession of the years and the flight
of ages : I shall not wholly die." It was a superb
claim ; and it has been ratified by the judgment of
history.

It would be, I am sure, superfluous, and I think
unbecoming, to say a single word here on what is
the primary duty of all citizens. But there is a
part of that duty in which the classics, and Horace
not least among them, are of direct, practical, and
daily help. Civilisation is bleeding at every pore.
To the faint-hearted it may seem as if the drain
on it will, before the end, be more than it can
bear. Well, the material fabric may perish, if the
soul survives. It is a task in which we all can
share to keep these wounds from becoming septic,
and to pour in fresh blood, so that the loss of so
many lives shall not end in the weakening or
poisoning of the national life itself. In its living,
unceasing, irreplaceable power to do this lies the
claim of poetry to our allegiance, and, among the
poets, the claim of the great classics.

# IX

# THE LAST GREAT ROMAN HISTORIAN

## (1921)

AMMIANUS MARCELLINUS has in this country long suffered undue and unfortunate neglect. No edition of him, so far as I know, has ever been produced in England. A translation executed nearly half a century ago by the late Professor C. D. Yonge, for Bohn's Classical Library, is, I think, not now readily accessible. Mr. Fisher, before he was called from the University of Sheffield to a larger and more laborious sphere, had bestowed much study on him; some of its results appeared in an article in the *Quarterly Review* for July 1918, which was last year republished in his volume of *Studies in History and Politics*. The Teubner text edited by Gardthausen in 1874–5 has long been out of print. An American scholar, Professor C. U. Clark, brought out at Berlin in 1910 the first volume of a revised text, and the second volume, completing the text and apparatus criticus, appeared in 1917; but they are difficult to obtain. It is good news that a text and translation are now being prepared by Mr. Clark for the Loeb Series; and it is to be hoped that this publication will not be long delayed.

He was actually better known here in the

seventeenth century than he is now.  Philemon
Holland, that miracle of industry who was called
the translator-general of the Elizabethan age—
best known now by his racy and delightfully read-
able version of Pliny's *Natural History*—translated
Ammianus also, as well as Livy, Suetonius,
Plutarch's *Moralia*, and Xenophon's *Cyropaedia*.
His folio *Ammianus* (1609) must have had a large
circulation, in view of the number of copies from
old libraries which come into the market.  One
of its interests for us is the fact that Milton, who
was born the year before its publication, un-
doubtedly read it while at Cambridge.  Holland,
who in 1609 was settled as a physician at Coventry,
had recently become also usher, or second master,
in the Free School there, of which he was afterwards head master.  He dedicated his *Ammianus*
to the Mayor and Corporation, "for divers respects," as he says in his preface.  One among
these respects is interesting enough to quote,
and might be a stimulus, or a lesson, to our local
education authorities.

"Secondly, the affectionate love that ye have
always borne to good literature, testified by
courteous entertainment of learned men ; by competent salaries allowed from time to time to such
professors as have peaceably, and with discreet
carriage, bestowed their talents among you ; by
exhibition given to poor scholars in the University ; by erecting also of late and maintaining
of a fair library, not exampled (without offence
to others be it spoken) in many cities of the
Realm."

The Corporation of Coventry responded to this
compliment by making Holland a grant of £4 ;

the equivalent, perhaps, in purchasing power of
£15 in 1914.[1]

It may not then be inappropriate to invite
fresh attention to Ammianus, and to attempt a
partial sketch of the picture drawn by him of the
age in which he lived. That period not only is in
itself of deep and tragic interest, but offers many
sinister analogies, as well as some encouraging
contrasts, to our own day. The matter at issue
was then, as it is now, nothing less than civilisation itself. The collapse of the Roman Empire
meant, partly as cause, partly as consequence,
the collapse of the whole fabric of the ancient
world. The joint process was irregular; it was
neither a case of steady decay, nor of sudden
extinction. But there was a turning-point which
was decisive; before which, hope was still possible; after which, there was no effective recovery.
The visible and dramatic symbol of that point is
the battle of Adrianople in A.D. 378. Within a
single generation thereafter, the Roman world in
its old sense had come to an end. Latin literature
had finished its course. The Latin organisation
of Western Europe had ceased effectively to exist,
and its provinces were being parcelled out in
barbarian kingdoms. The reins of government in
the eastern and western halves of the *orbis
Romanus*, of which Theodosius was the last single
ruler, dangled in the hands of his two children,
one of whom was a puppet and the other an idiot.
Rome had been stormed and sacked by Alaric's
Goths with their Hun auxiliaries. St. Augustine
had written, in the *De Civitate Dei*, the epitaph

[1] This figure is based on the conclusions reached by Sir Charles
Firth, *Cromwell's Army*, pp. 188-189.

of the ancient world. Thenceforward, though the total darkness did not fall until the sixth century or even later, we are in the deepening twilight of the Dark Ages.

The few facts known about Ammianus, all or nearly all of which are derived from his own *History*, may be summarised in order to define him for the moment. He was of Greek birth and a native of Antioch. As a young man he was enrolled in the Protectores Domestici, a *corps d'élite* of the Imperial Guard. He served under Ursicinus, Master of the Cavalry, in the eastern provinces, then in Italy and Gaul, and again in the East from A.D. 350 onward. He took part in the Persian campaign of Julian, in which he narrowly escaped capture by the enemy. From his knowledge of machine-guns and the evident interest he takes in them, it seems that he may have acted as an artillery officer. He apparently retired from active service soon after, and settled down in a literary society at Rome, where he wrote his *History*. It ends with the year 378, and there is no allusion in it to any date later than 390,[1] when it was probably published.

His faults as a writer are such as might be expected in a retired officer, *miles quondam et Graecus*,[2] to quote his own concluding words, whose early education had been very incomplete. He had entered the service young, and Latin was an acquired language for him. He is capable of using it with extraordinary force and skill. He can be terse, he can be eloquent: in many vivid descriptive touches like *dies umectus et decolor*,[3] in not a few magnificent phrases like *triumphaturas*

---

[1] xxvi. 5, 14.    [2] xxxi. 16, 9.    [3] xvi. 2, 10.

*aquilas et vexilla victricia,*[1] he recaptures the authentic Roman speech. But in his efforts at writing good Latin he constantly falls back on phrases which he found in books; and he belongs to the Middle Ages in his habit not only of dragging in quotations from Cicero or Virgil at any opportunity—I have noted more than fifty of these—but of copying their language as nearly as possible instead of expressing his meaning straightforwardly. His *flosculi Tulliani*[2] were no doubt greatly appreciated by his immediate circle, but they are a sore trial to the modern reader. Further, he is fond of making long and often quite irrelevant digressions. He was interested in what then passed for science, both physical and moral; and he will, on a very slight pretext, break off his narrative to discuss, on the one hand, the causes of earthquakes, pestilences, eclipses, rainbows, and other celestial phenomena,[3] and on the other, the various kinds of divination, the doctrine of the daemon or tutelary spirit, or the existence of a power called Adrastia or Nemesis and operating from the circle of the moon.[4] A careful student of Livy, as his imitations, not always unsuccessful, of the Livian period prove,[5] he did not take to heart the weighty sentence in which his great predecessor had warned against this way of writing history : *Nihil minus quaesitum a principio huius operis videri potest, quam ut plus iusto ab rerum ordine declinarem, varietatibusque distin-*

---

[1] xvi. 12, 12.          [2] xxix. 1, 11.
[3] xvii. 7, 9–14 ; xix. 4 ; xx. 3 ; xx. 11, 26–30.
[4] xxi. 1, 7–14 ; xxi. 14, 2–5 ; xiv. 11, 25.
[5] Good instances may be found in the opening paragraphs of xiv. and xxiv. Others are frequent.

*guendo opere ut legentibus velut deverticula amoena
et requiem animo meo quaererem.*[1] The *deverticula* of
Ammianus are not without some indirect value as
throwing light on what modern jargon would
call the mentality both of the historian and of
his age. But they have done grave injury to his
reputation.[2]

These faults are in the main superficial; they
are those of what he modestly calls his *mediocre
ingenium*.[3] His merits, which are fundamental,
must be weighed apart from them. We may
hardly go so far as to say with Henri Valois, his
first competent and careful editor, that he
challenges comparison with any of the greatest
writers of history, *mihi quidem summis quibusque
historiae scriptoribus comparandus videtur.* But we
must agree with the grave and considered praise
of Gibbon: "sincere," "modest," "loyal to his
superior officers," "copious and authentic," "an
accurate and faithful guide, without the prejudices
and passions which usually affect the mind of a
contemporary." His own words, "miles et
Graecus," might be paraphrased without injustice
by saying that he was an officer and a gentleman;
and on deliberate judgment he may be given a
place among the great Roman historians, of whom
he was in any case certainly the last.

The extant portion of his *History* covers the
twenty-five years from 353 to 378 A.D. The first

---

[1] Liv. ix. 17.

[2] It is fair to observe—and the remark applies to all ancient
writings—that nowadays such digressions would not be incorporated in the text of a history, but relegated to notes or ap-
pendices, where, whatever their value might be, they would at all
events not be felt as irritating interruptions.

[3] xvi. 1, 1 ; cf. xxvii. 11, 1.

thirteen books are lost; they began with the accession of Nerva, and thus covered more than 250 years. Much the greater part of that period must have only been treated in very brief summary; yet if the lost books were recovered, they would no doubt add materially to our knowledge of the long period for which we have to depend so much on the wretched authors of the *Historia Augusta*. We may follow his example by a rapid and cursory sketch of the change that had passed over the Roman world during the Middle Empire, starting from the majestic phrase which Gibbon made the title of the second chapter of the *Decline and Fall*, "Of the Union and Internal Prosperity of the Roman Empire in the Age of the Antonines." The spectacle there presented to us is of an organised empire extending from the Clyde to the Euphrates, from Hungary to the Sahara, based on broad foundations, civilised, prosperous, well administered, seemingly secure. Throughout it there was, with hardly an exception, profound internal peace. Agriculture, industry, and commerce flourished. The population of the lands within Roman government exceeded anything reached afterwards until the nineteenth century. Wealth was lavished on public improvements and philanthropic institutions. The armies were well equipped and disciplined. Civil administration was in the hands of an able and highly organised civil service. Education was being extended; provincial universities were founded and attended by crowds of students. The arts of sculpture, music, architecture, were at a high level. The Roman world had settled down to take its ease. External causes of collapse were distant. The intermittent Persian wars on a fluctuating frontier had little result, except indeed for the cumulative drain of vital and material resources. The northern peril was always there in the background, as it had always been since the days of Herodotus.[1] But it was no greater than it had been in the times of Marius or Germanicus. No material impression was made on the Empire by the barbarians during 250 years after the destruction by the Germans of the 17th, 18th, and 19th legions. It was more than a century later still before any Roman territory was formally ceded to an enemy.[2]

The causes of decay lay deep within. There was a gradual atrophy of intellectual energy and of public spirit. The instinct of self-government was lost. Free institutions withered away. The government of the Antonines rested on precarious foundations. The good emperors came to an end. From the beginning of the third century onwards there was a constant succession of civil wars and military mutinies. The burden of armaments is spoken of in quite modern terms. We read, under the year 361, of the institution of compulsory military training throughout the provinces, of immense pressure to accumulate equipment, and of the outcry that rose "from every rank and pro-fession" at the intolerable tax of requisitions for uniforms, arms, stores of food, draught-animals, and military engines.[3] The cumulative drain and dislocation were immense—*parabantur nihilo minus externorum atque civilium instrumenta bellorum*—and alongside of this went an aggregation of the population in huge cities and exhaustion of the

[1] Herod. v. 3.
[2] xxv. 9, 9.
[3] xxi. 6, 1.

permanent sources of wealth. The first great shock came in A.D. 250 with the Gothic invasion of the Balkan Peninsula. In the same year began the Black Death which raged for fifteen years and was said to have carried off half the population of the empire. A Jacquerie in Gaul, a revolt of the agricultural serfs, permanently crippled the West. Predatory bands of Franks and Allemanni wandered almost unchecked over Spain, north-west Africa, and Italy. The empire seemed going to pieces. It was saved by the great Illyrian emperors, Claudius and his successors. Aurelian re-established the eastern frontier and organised the barrier-province of Dacia. Central Germany was effectually brought under control by Probus. At the triumph of Diocletian in 302 the strength and prosperity of the empire seemed fully restored, and the new monarchy created by him destined to a long and prosperous career. But it was far otherwise. Diocletian's triumph was the last ever celebrated in Rome ; and his new monarchy was ill-starred from the beginning.

From Diocletian the new monarchy passed, after a series of destructive civil wars, to the feeble and bloody house of Constantine. As the first Christian emperor, and as founder of the new Rome at the strategic centre of the Roman world, Constantine became crowned with a legendary halo. But his work was fatal to the Empire and to what remained of the Roman tradition. *Infirmator imperii*, the phrase used of him by Dante,[1] is the exact truth. Bureaucratic tyranny became absolute. The armies were deliberately made inefficient as a safeguard against civil wars

[1] *De Monarchia*, ii. 13.

Administration was barbarised by a criminal law of unexampled ferocity. From no rational conviction, and in no spirit of either faith or hope, Christianity was made the state religion. Government loaded itself with the weight of blood-stained theological controversy ; and the Church in return took over the hideous inheritance of persecution from the savage penal code of the empire.

The reactionary policy of Constantine's nephew Julian was futile in its object and merely disastrous in its results. With him the house of Constantine became extinct. Under his successors, the joint-emperors Valentinian and Valens—the few months of the stop-gap reign of Jovian are negligible—the beginning of the end came.

This is the period recorded in the extant work of Ammianus. He records it with a sincerity, an absence of prejudice or passion, which rise at points to a tragic greatness. He is still too often thought of as though he were merely the biographer of Julian : a misconception which is inherited from the time when the records of ancient civilisation were the province of Christian theologians, and civil was subordinated to ecclesiastical history. The story of Julian's career is only one episode in his picture of a whole age and its movement. It is elsewhere that he rises most conspicuously to the height of his argument : particularly in two episodes, one at the end of his work, the other, as it happens, almost at the beginning of the extant portion. This latter is the vivid and dramatic story of the end of Gallus Caesar [1] ; the net slowly closing round him, his arrest, his execution by night, and the wild ride of Apodemius from Pola

[1] xiv. 11 ; xv. 1.

to Milan carrying the scarlet shoes of the murdered
man to lay before Constantius; with the two
figures, to left and right as one might say in the
piece, one sinister, the other innocently tragic:
the eunuch Eusebius, Provost of the Bedchamber,
the *Eminence Grise* who was the real master of the
world, and the empress, "still human on that
dizzy height," *in culmine tam celso humana*.[1] It is
an illuminating and unforgettable picture, seen as
it were by a flashlight, of the household fury that
tore into the entrails of the wretched imperial
house.

The other is a scene on a larger canvas; the
narrative of the great disaster of A.D. 378. Its
structure is elaborately skilful. It opens with
portents ; the *fides clara praesagiorum*,[2] which impressed even this cool-headed and experienced
official, sets the dramatic keynote. Then follows
a sketch of the loosening of the northern nations,
urged on by vast movements and migrations in
Central Asia, and of the new Mongol terror, the
hordes of Alans and Huns who were pouring into
Europe. From this, the historian leads us on to
watch the Imperial Government making every
possible blunder. A great Gothic host was forced
into Thrace and supplied with Roman arms by
the treachery and incompetence of the provincial
officials. The mining population of the province,
oppressed and misgoverned, joined them by
thousands. The old Cimbric and Marcomannic
perils were renewed and outdone. Picked troops
were drafted from all the provinces until the whole

---

[1] xxi. 6, 4. She died soon after, "as good as she was
beautiful."
[2] **xxxi**. 1, 1.

M

military strength of the empire was concentrated
in one magnificent army. Then we have the
account of the alarm and irresolution of Fritigern
and the fatal decision of Valens to force a battle.
On the morning of that burning August day, and
even when, in the early afternoon, the Roman
army came in sight of the great Gothic waggon-
lager, a complete and crushing Roman victory
was on both sides thought inevitable. *Dis aliter
visum.* In a paroxysm of mingled terror and
fury, the Gothic foot and the Hun horse swarmed
out and flung themselves desperately on the
imperial army, still partly in column of march,
and flagging from heat and thirst. The flanking
Roman cavalry was broken and swept away at the
first charge, and the whole of the infantry, without
time to deploy, was jammed into a helpless mass
and, as at Cannae, stood to be slaughtered. When
the hot moonless night fell, more than two-thirds
of that splendid army, the emperor among them,
lay dead on the field. From Cannae, as earlier
from the Allia, Rome had recovered herself; but
Adrianople remained unavenged. "The fall of
the Roman Empire," Gibbon says, "may justly be
dated from the reign of Valens."

The Roman Empire fell; and outside of the
Roman Empire there was no home. It was to its
inhabitants a lit house surrounded by black darkness; or, to those among them who hated it and
would fain have renounced it, a prison out of
which there was no escape. When the house
collapsed, when the prison walls crumbled, it
seemed to men, not to St. Augustine only, that
the end of the world was surely near. The
prestige and glamour of the world-empire, with

all that it meant, were still overwhelming. The Germanic and Gothic nations regarded it with mixed fascination and fear—German troops had to be levied on the undertaking that they should not be sent south of the Alps[1]—but they kept being sucked by an irresistible fascination into the charmed circle. The Persian satrap of Corduene contemplated desertion to the Roman side, not as a traitor nor for material profit, but from his passion for Western culture, *dulcedine liberalium studiorum illectus :* as a hostage in Syria in his boyhood he had tasted Graeco-Roman civilisation, and found he could not live without it.[2] The name of Rome remained magical. It was known through the world as the Eternal City[3]: and it is particularly noticeable that the name became even more prevalent after the transference of the centre of government to Milan and the foundation of the New Rome of Constantine. Rome was *domina et regina, urbs venerabilis, caput mundi, victura cum seculis, urbs sacratissima, templum mundi totius.*[4] No less in the wearers of the purple there remained a sense of imperial duty and mission.

> Their shoulders held the sky suspended,
> They stood, and earth's foundations stay.

Julian says when dying, *Ubicunque velut imperiosa parens obiecit respublica, steti fundatus.*[5] We find the same feeling even in Valentinian, whose thin veneer of culture—*scribens decore*, says

---

[1] xx. 4, 4.     [2] xvii. 6, 20.
[3] It is so named eleven times in Ammianus.
[4] xv. 6, 6; xiv. 6, 5; xiv. 6, 23; xxvi. 1, 14; xxvii. 3, 3; xvii. 4, 12.
[5] xxv. 3, 18.

Ammianus, *venusteque pingens et fingens*—was overlaid on a brutal savage.  He announces his purpose of associating Gratian in the imperial dignity
with the grave and impressive words, *in augustum
sumere commilitium paro.*[1]  That *commilitium*, fellowship in service, was no mere phrase.  The burden
of empire was not lightly taken up or lightly
carried.  Its maintenance was still the highest
and all-inclusive duty.  Even yet, prolonged periods
of external tranquillity sometimes raised anew,
like a phantom, the old tradition of the *Pax
Romana*.  Of one of these periods, in a striking
phrase—the more notable for us because Milton
transferred it almost bodily into his *Nativity Ode*—
Ammianus says, *Quievere nationes omnes immobiles
ac si quodam caduceo leniente mundum.*[2]  "No war,
or battle's sound, was heard the world around . . .
and kings sat still with awful eye, as if they surely
knew their sovran lord was by."

It is not by detached pictures, however vivid
and tragic, nor is it by the reflections of an historian,
that we can estimate the whole set and movement
of an age.  Both are but lights thrown on particular incidents or aspects of what is an immense
and continuous organic life.  What Napoleon
named as the besetting sin of generals, *réunir les
faits pour en former des tableaux*,[3] is equally true of
historians.  Ammianus' importance for our study
rests very largely on the incidental—one might
almost say, the accidental—information which he
gives at a hundred points on the whole life of his
age, both on its material and on its intellectual or
spiritual side.  Except in the unlucky digressions,

[1] xxvii. 6, 8.  [2] xxv. 4, 14.
[3] Under date February 23, 1814.

he never theorises. He is almost as detached as Thucydides himself in the matter of drawing morals. This quality goes with, if it does not lie at the base of, his remarkable power of characterisation; he makes the figures in his history live, because he is himself a translucent medium. One may quote here the striking words of Seeck. After mentioning the faults and weaknesses of Ammianus, "Dagegen besitzt er," he goes on, "in der Schilderung menschlicher Charaktere eine Meisterschaft welche in der ganzen antiken Litteratur kaum ihresgleichen hat, und ihn trotz seiner grossen Schwächen den ersten Geschichtschreibern aller Zeiten anreiht."

A word must be said here on his attitude towards Christianity. In religious doctrine as such he appears to take little interest; in religious controversy he takes no side. Himself a pagan, he speaks of the Christian faith, *religionem absolutam et simplicem*,[1] with entire respect. He quotes, simply in the way of record, Julian's saying, *Nullas infestas hominibus bestias ut sunt sibi ferales plerique Christianorum*.[2] But of Julian's sarcasm he yields no trace; and he departs so far from his usual detachment as to censure twice over the edict closing the schools of grammar and rhetoric to Christian teachers.[3] He records without any comment the Christian riots in Rome at the election of Pope Damasus, when 137 dead bodies were taken out of a single church.[4] He deliberately pauses to note and praise the simple life of the provincial bishops.[5] His own standpoint, far in

[1] xxi. 16, 18.
[3] xxii. 10, 7 ; xxv. 4, 20.
[5] xxvii. 3, 14–15.

[2] xxii. 5, 3.
[4] xxvii. 3, 13.

advance of his age, though very likely shared with
him by the best of the trained and educated
official class, was that of absolute religious toleration. It was one not recovered for many ages.
"Even the intellectual perception of the value of
toleration had not yet dawned upon the world," the
historian of seventeenth-century England writes
with a just insight.[1] It was a doctrine not formu-
lated till the eighteenth century and hardly brought
into practice before the nineteenth. Ammianus'
ideal is the policy which he attributes to one of
the so-called Christian emperors : *Inter religionum
diversitates medius stetit, nec quemquam inquietavit,
neque ut hoc coleretur imperavit aut illud.*[2] But this
is not, as it was with Valentinian, mere oppor-
tunism, the attitude of "Why can't you leave
things alone?" For Ammianus is fundamentally
religious. In one noble phrase, *perpetuum numen
verique eius cultores,*[3] he includes both the old and
the new faiths, and rises to a higher synthesis like
that seen as in a vision by Akbar, that which
inspired the great humanists, that in which many
minds now find their anchorage.

The remarkable phrase *seculi progressio,*[4] once
used incidentally by Ammianus, has been taken,
pressing it rather beyond what it will bear, to
mean that he held a doctrine of human progress
in the modern sense.[5] Such a doctrine was unknown to the ancient world. It was developed in
the eighteenth century from the hints given by

---

[1] S. R. Gardiner, vol. vii. p. 158 (under date of 1629).
[2] xxx. 9, 5.      [3] xxvii. 3, 15.      [4] xviii. 7, 7.
[5] "He believes," Professor Bury wrote a good many years
ago. "in progress and the enlightenment of his age." But this
*obiter dictum*, in a note to Gibbon, must be taken with some
qualification ; see in particular the introductory chapter of *The
Idea of Progress.*

earlier humanism, and was dominant during the greater part of the nineteenth. In its earlier inferential form it is perhaps most strikingly expressed by Gibbon (1781) in the celebrated sentence with which he concludes his 38th chapter : "We may acquiesce in the pleasing conclusion that every age of the world has increased, and still increases, the real wealth, the happiness, the knowledge, and perhaps the virtue, of the human race." Half a century later, the pleasing conclusion had passed into a dogmatic belief. It lay at the roots of Liberalism ; it may be called the main motive force of the Victorian age. The phrase of Ammianus cannot be matched in classical literature, nor, I think, is there any trace before it of the belief or theory which it has been thought to imply, not even as a reaction against the common doctrine of progressive deterioration. But in the fourth century many new ideas and theories were in the air. It was a time, like the present, in which loss both of hard thinking power, and of imagination—which has been suggestively defined as the faculty of seeing and tracing consequences—was accompanied by intense receptivity and by a feverish pursuit of short-cuts alike in thought and in practice.

It was on its military side that the *progressio seculi* was most obvious. The incomparable Roman infantry had ceased to exist. Field-fortification was developed ; and Ammianus speaks, in terms which sound curiously familiar, of the German underground trench-fighting and its formidable difficulty.[1] Artillery had developed into an arm of great importance. To realise what

[1] xvii. 1, 8.

this meant, it is legitimate or even necessary to think in modern terms of the military engines then used, making of course due allowance for the difference in range and destructive power between guns using only elastic or torsional force and those using explosives. These only came much later; gunpowder, or its equivalent, is spoken of as a new invention towards the end of the ninth century. Ammianus describes [1] the heavy guns, *ballistae*, each mounted on an ironclad barbette; the field-artillery, which could be moved, though with some difficulty, on the actual battlefield, and could be used effectively even against the *ballistae;* and the lighter machine-guns which were readily shifted from point to point. The *scorpio*, a weapon of great power, could be trained in any direction by a single gunner. Incendiary bombs were largely used; also the *malleolus* or hand-trench-bomb with which we have in recent years become terribly familiar. The flame-thrower was a later invention, and seems to have been developed almost entirely for naval action. Fleets of the *vehicula publica* ordinarily employed in postal and passenger service were used on a large scale for hurrying up reinforcements, or even transferring a whole army from one front to another.[2] Yet the military weakness of the empire tended to increase. The armies were manned and largely officered by barbarians. No national army in the modern sense was possible, because the sense of nationality had been lost. The New Empire was neither a nation nor a league of nations; it was international in name, anti-national in spirit, an administrative organism resting on a caste system, hostile to the

---

[1] xxiii. 4 ; xix. 5, 1 ; xxiv. 4, 17, and 28.    [2] xxi. 13, 7.

instinct and practice of self-government, and held
together by laws of frightful severity.

The two things, decay of self-government and
cruelty of law, reacted on one another. As far
back as the later Republic, popular government
had completely failed in its task. It was set aside
in the interest of efficiency. Efficiency was to a
large extent secured; but government was
launched on the slippery slope on which there
was no stopping, still less any returning. Under
the lesser Antonines, Septimius Severus and his
son Antoninus Caracalla, trial by jury finally disappeared. That was a more important thing than
it may seem. The abuses of corrupt juries were
the reason or the pretext; and these abuses were
real and grave. But the result was uncontrolled
criminal jurisdiction of officials. Legal trial was
superseded by administrative process. Death
after torture could be inflicted for any crime; and
the list of crimes was continually lengthened. But
beyond that list, the monstrous invention of *stellionatus* covered any act which was not legally
criminal. *Poena stellionatus nulla legitima est, cum
neque legitimum crimen sit*, are the words of Ulpian.[1]
With dreadful monotony in Ammianus comes,
every few pages, a sickening record of tortures
and hideous deaths set down almost without comment. Burning alive was the common punishment.
*Flammis iussit exuri : vivus exustus est : ad interitum
tortos incendit*, is the summary record of innumerable cases.[2] There was no redress; *de fumo in flam-*

---

[1] Digest, xlvii. 20, 3. "There is no occasion," he grimly
adds, "to enumerate instances."

[2] xxvii. 7, 6; xiv. 7, 17; xxix. 5, 50. Dozens and scores of
similar citations could be made. The accounts are almost too
horrible to read.

*mam*,[1] in an awfully literal sense, was the probable
event of any appeal. Two provincials who had
ventured to carry complaints of extortion against
the Count of Africa to the Imperial Court had
their tongues cut out there.[2] A boy, the son of
an officer of high rank, was sentenced to exile for
dabbling in magic. He appealed to Valentinian in
person. The result is told in three words: *cecidit
carnificis manu.*[3]

These accusations of practising magic were an
outstanding feature of the time. The craving to
get into communication with the dead, and to
force secrets out of dark unseen powers, ran like
a fever through all classes, especially the intel-
lectuals and the rich. It was condemned alike by
the Church and by the civil authority, but it grew
none the less; and it was held to be public policy
to stamp it out by treating it as a capital offence.
Such a policy lent itself at once to the trade of
the informer. The reign of terror at Rome in 368,
and in the cities of Syria in 371, can hardly be
paralleled except by the records of the last months
of the Revolutionary Tribunal.[4] Trials were an
open farce; the batches of accused, herded in
pestilential dungeons, were swept off indiscrimi-
nately to the scaffold. There were daily execu-
tions of prisoners already crippled by tortures.
The word "witchcraft" had only to be spoken to
rouse a frenzy of terror. *Unde factum est per
orientales provincias ut omnes metu similium exure-
rent libraria omnia.*[5] Humane learning and inherited culture were crushed, never to be restored,
in the capital of the east.

[1] xxviii. 1, 26.    [2] xxviii. 6, 20.    [3] xxviii. 1, 26.
[4] xxviii. 1 ; xxix. 1 and 2.    [5] xxix. 2, 4.

Yet civilised life went on; and there is abundant evidence in Ammianus of its continued brilliance. Rome was still the great social centre. The elaborate account he gives of its wealth and luxury[1] is to be read with some reserve; it is rhetorical and artificial, and he exchanges the pen of the historian for the brush of the satirist. But certain facts incidentally mentioned by him are significant. Civic improvements continued to be made, like the clearing away of the shops clustered round temples or churches, and the erection of the great obelisk in the Circus.[2] The decoration and machinery of theatres were increasingly elaborate.[3] Public health was scientifically guarded; the precautions taken against infectious diseases, though they probably did not extend beyond the well-to-do classes, read quite like those of modern times.[4] Music was much cultivated; and the manufacture both of organs and of stringed instruments comparable in size to pianos is particularly noted.[5] But the vast majority of citizens lived only for frivolity and excitement. The public libraries were closed for lack of readers, where they were not perishing from neglect or deliberately destroyed. Frivolous and immoral books on the one hand, spiritualistic and magical treatises on the other, were the only reading of the leisured and educated classes, *detestantes ut venena doctrinas.* Gambling and betting on races were the main occupations: *nihil serium agi Romae permittunt.*[6]

---

[1] xiv. 6.   [2] xxvii. 9, 10 ; xvi. 4, 14–15.
[3] xiv. 6, 19–20 ; xvi. 12, 57 ; xxvi. 6, 15.   [4] xiv. 6, 23.
[5] xiv. 6, 18, lyrae ad speciem carpentorum ingentes. Cf. *Anth. Pal.* vii. 571.
[6] xiv. 6, 26 ; xxviii. 4, 14.

Elsewhere than at Rome, similar wealth and luxury are mentioned, as also immense traffic and commerce. The streets of Antioch by night were as bright as day.[1] At Alexandria were great schools of music, mathematics, and medicine.[2] Oribasius, the contemporary of Ammianus, is the last great name in the history of ancient medical science, and continued the high tradition of Galen in the age of the Antonines.[3] A caravan route from Bactria to China, in constant use, brought the Far East into touch with Europe.[4] The use of *serica*, Indian muslins, was common even among the lowest classes.[5] The embassies from Ceylon, *ab usque Serendivis*, sank into Milton's imagination and reappear in the most gorgeous passage of the *Paradise Regained*.[6] The great September fair at Batnae on the Euphrates was stocked with wares from India and China, and drew traders from all parts of the world.[7] No one who reads Ammianus, however cursorily, can fail to be struck by the number of references to the immense prestige which still, outside as well as inside the empire, surrounded the imperial person, the fabric of Roman administration, and the discipline and equipment of the armies.[8] His vivid picture of

[1] xiv. 1, 9; xiv. 8, 8.    [2] xxii. 16, 17-18.

[3] Through Arabic translations, his works had an important influence on medical science and practice in the rich civilisation of the Khalifat. Like Ammianus, he was an adherent of the ancient faith. It was he who brought back to Julian from Delphi the well-known lines announcing the extinction of the oracle, which may be called the swan-song of the old religion.

[4] xxiii. 6, 60.    [5] xxiii. 6, 67.

[6] xxii. 7, 10; *P. R.* iv. 74-76.    [7] xiv. 3, 3.

[8] For this last, see particularly xvi. 12, 12; xviii. 2, 17; xxvii. 2, 5, and 5, 3; xxviii. 5, 3; xxix. 5, 15; xxx. 5, 13; xxxi. 10, 9, and 14. In the phrase cited above, p. 163, *triumphaturas aquilas et vexilla victricia*, the voice of Rome speaks.

the state entry of Constantius into Rome in A.D.
356[1]—his single visit to the ancient capital—might
be thought of as symbolic of that faded yet still
imposing splendour.

But it was the brilliance that preceded dissolution. There was a steady loss of both intellectual
and moral fibre. Civilisation, while it was being
sapped by barbarian infiltration, and by an economic system which oppressed labour, drained
capital, and hampered industry, was sick of a
more inward and more incurable disease. The
virtue had gone out of it. Nerve and impulse
failed. The *caries vetustatis*[2]—perhaps the most
striking single phrase used by Ammianus—had
eaten in. Already the sombre words of Fredegar,
actually written two centuries later in the heart
of the Dark Ages, *Mundus iam senescit,*[3] might
have been uttered. *Nihil multa et nefanda perpessis
hominibus praeter lacrimas supererat et terrores, ubi
et praeteritorum recordatio erat acerba et exspectatio
tristior impendentium.*[4]

I have spoken of barbarian infiltration, not
barbarian invasion. Invasions of the empire on
a large scale had in fact hitherto been quite
exceptional, and their results even when most
disastrous had been transitory. But groups and
even whole tribes kept continually trickling in;
sometimes forcibly, sometimes by express or tacit
agreement, often by actual invitation. Gradually
the distinction between the *orbis Romanus* and the
outer world became effaced. The empire was
peopled throughout by mixed races which did not
crystallise. The new blood helped to keep up

[1] xvi. 10, 4–17.  [2] xvi. 2, 1.
[3] *Scriptt. Rer. Franc.* ii. 414.  [4] xxv. 4, 25.

fighting power. But for civil administration, on which all else finally rested, no new blood was to be had. By the same sort of instinct, which made them fear and avoid towns, *ut circumdata retiis busta*,[1] the northern races shrank from the complex mysteries of government. In 363, the Frank Malarich refused the offered command of Gaul and Illyricum on this express account.[2] Thus even when the western empire had ceased to be anything but a name, the Ostrogothic kingdom of Italy, the Vandal kingdom of Africa, the Visigothic kingdom of Spain, had no roots, no principle of growth, and went to pieces at a touch. "Die letzte Phase des römischen Staats," Mommsen wrote in 1885, "ist bezeichnet durch dessen Barbarisirung und speciell dessen Germanisirung."[3] Thirty-six years later, the words are even more illuminating and impressive than they were then. One of the darkest facts which come out in the narrative of Ammianus is that the Roman word could no longer be trusted. Assassinations of hostile chiefs or princes under safe-conduct, even at banquets to which they had been invited as guests, wholesale massacres of forces which had surrendered under express assurance of safety, are chronicled over and over again as common incidents: sometimes without comment; *clam quia non potuit aperte*[4]: sometimes with uneasy and unconvinced excuses[5]: in one of the most shocking instances, with actual approval, as *consilium prudens* and *efficacia salutaris et velox*.[6] Such was the

---

[1] xvi. 2, 12.        [2] xxv. 8, 11 ; 10, 6.
[3] *Römische Geschichte*, Band v. Buch viii. 4 *sub finem*.
[4] xxx. 7, 7 ; cf. xxvii. 10, 4.        [5] xxviii. 5, 4–7.
[6] xxxi. 16, 8.

deplorable effect of lowered public conscience upon an officer and a gentleman.

> "Public reason just,
> Honour and Empire with revenge enlarg'd
> Compels me now to do what I abhor":
> So spake the Fiend, and with necessity
> The Tyrant's plea, excus'd his devilish deeds.

But once at least, following his own better nature and discarding his usual reticence, he calls on the Romans of old, *si qua vita digressis est dolor*, to mourn over the infamy of their descendants.[1]

The leaven was insufficient: it was overwhelmed by the brute matter. Rome could do, and did, wonders, but she could not really *urbem facere quod prius orbis erat*, incorporate and civilise the world. The task was too great for a nation which was losing both vital force and racial identity. The achievements of the Illyrian emperors were the last attempt made to do so But the ground kept crumbling under their feet. A little later, the picking up of the pieces, *colligere provinciae fragmenta*, is named as all that was possible in Gaul. A creeping paralysis came over the empire, and at last it succumbed.

This is not an occasion to labour the lessons to be drawn from the tragic and absorbing record of a period which has so many points in common with our own. But there are two points on which I may perhaps be permitted to say a word; for they do not, superficially at least, arise directly out of the sketch I have attempted to give, and they are both of great interest. I will merely state the questions, and not venture to supply answers to them.

---

[1] xxx. 1, 19 ; cf. xxix. 6, 5.

The first is, could education have saved the empire? It may be doubted. In the second century it had done all it could. If it be objected that the kind of education then organised, as we have it set forth in the Institution of Quintilian, was faulty or misdirected, the answer is that the best minds of the time did not think so. The object aimed at, the production of good citizens, is unchallengeable. The methods for attaining it are quite as much the subject of controversy now as they were then. Each age works according to its own nature; in education as in other matters, neither theory nor practice can be antedated. The theory and practice of the Empire represent the problem and its provisional solution according to the knowledge available, and the strength of belief in it needed to convert it from theoretic doctrine into actual motive force. System is little more than the codification of usage. While it is true that supply tends, often powerfully, to create demand, there is no such thing as permanent un-demanded supply. People get, on the whole, the sort of education they want. It is because they do not know what they want, or do not want it enough, that they are dissatisfied with what they get. Education is a function of the social organism; national education is, both in kind and degree, the consequence rather than the cause of national vitality. But I will not pursue this subject further. I turn to the second question: What was the cause of the decay of the Roman Empire?

In the lecture on Decadence by Lord Balfour, republished in the volume entitled *Essays: Speculative and Political,* he reviews the sources which

have been assigned for it. Chief among these he
names :

(1) Depopulation. It is doubtful how far the
fact of depopulation is established. What is clear
is a relative depopulation of rural areas and small
country towns, and an increasing aggregation in
large cities. This means, as we need not go
abroad to verify, that the equilibrium of civilisation becomes more precarious.

(2) The institution of slavery, the brutalities of
the gladiatorial shows, the gratuitous distribution
of food to urban mobs. These he dismisses,
rightly I think, as inadequate causes, though they
may have been and probably were contributory.

(3) The growth under bureaucratic pressure of
a caste system, to which he justly assigns great
importance, not only in itself, but as bringing
about failure in the power of the social organism
to assimilate alien elements, which, he adds, it
became too feeble either to absorb or to expel.

In a note to the lecture, Lord Balfour further
lays stress on the evidence for a general degra-
dation in the productiveness of the soil in the
Mediterranean countries during the period under
review, and suggests that this purely physical
cause has been too much overlooked. Certainly
it was to a purely physical cause, the desiccation
of Central Asia, that the epoch of the invasions,
from the fourth century onward, was immediately
due.

But we may ask how far decay may have been
due not to any or all of the causes usually assigned,
but to something deeper and less under human
control ; namely, the exhaustion of a particular
breed, and the disappearance with it of a vital

N

element by infusion of which the Roman character and civilisation had been created. We know that throughout the sphere of organic life, alike in the vegetable and the animal world, strains of unique quality appear unaccountably and gradually die out or are reabsorbed. The reabsorption can be delayed, but cannot be altogether prevented by all that human ingenuity can do in selection of breeders and segregation of recessives. The history of the progeny of the Darley Arabian and his more famous descendant Eclipse, and of that of the Ribston apple tree, are well-known instances of a general principle. Even in the inorganic world something analogous takes place. Not only does micro-photography reveal the "fatigue" of metals, the breakdown of their crystalline structure whether through effects of external environment or the silent processes of internal strain, but metals themselves are in course of time degraded : silver becomes lead. It seems true of the human race that certain very subtle admixtures of blood, such as can neither be fully analysed nor purposely produced, are the condition of marked racial or national distinction. The determining element may be very small in amount and yet, like chromium in steel, may change the structure and quality of the whole resulting product of the nation or race. Some such alloy, or some such hybridisation, seems to have produced the outstanding human breeds. The gradual loss of its virtue in any strain, whether by mere wastage or by progressive dilution, is an insensible and in the main an uncontrollable process. But definite events may visibly accelerate it. Among these are changes in the social structure to which a particular strain does not readily react. Among them also are prolonged and widespread epidemics. The two Black Deaths of A.D. 165–170 and 250–265 had a large share in bringing about the decay of the Empire, not so much by actual and numerable depopulation as by exhaustion of the strain which gave its character to the Roman race. Each fresh rally became more laborious as the continual blood-tax and brain-tax of world-rule grew heavier. There were not Romans left to carry on the work of Rome.

# X

## THE CLASSICS

Presidential Address to the Classical Association, at Bristol, April 11, 1923.

The office which I have held for the past year is a high honour; it also carries a large responsibility. I can best thank the Classical Association for their choice of me to fill it, not by words of formulary gratitude, but by recording my own belief, and reinforcing what is, I think, their own growing conviction, that the position of the Association has never been stronger than it is now; that the studies which it exists in order to promote, to improve, to extend, and to secure are advancing steadily in the recognition they command, in the methods by which they are handled, and in the spirit in which they are pursued.

A turning-point was reached, after long effort, two or three years ago. The tide has begun to flow. If we have to meet new difficulties, they can be overcome like difficulties in other spheres. Faith, hope, love, and work—that I may quote from the remarkable speech made by the Chancellor of the Exchequer in the House of Commons in his recent survey of the national position—these are the keynotes, these the foundation stones. And if it be more than ever needful to bear in mind how far short we are of our ideals, if we should adopt as our motto the *Nil actum credens dum quid superesset agendum* of Julius Caesar, if we are indeed only at the beginning of a task which has no end, of a mission which has no limit, yet the time has come when we need no longer fight rearguard actions or feel ourselves supporters of a lost cause and an impossible loyalty. In this last year our membership has been substantially increased. Three more branches have been formed, bringing up the total number in England and Wales to seventeen ; and it is noteworthy that eight of these seventeen have been founded in the last four years, as against nine in the ten years between the creation of the Classical Association and the outbreak of the Great War. With a little more effort, the network of branches will effectively cover the whole country, and provide a mechanism for assembling local effort, for creating local interest, for a closer association of scattered teachers and students and scholars. Material increase has been accompanied by a growth in diffused vitality. The work of the central body will become more and more to guide and advise, to stimulate and co-ordinate, a movement in progress throughout the nation.

It will not, then, be inappropriate to-day to revert to first principles and to make the Classics themselves the subject of this address. I will ask you, both those who, as members of the Association, are concerned to promote the growth and maintain the well-being of classical studies, and those others to whom these studies are a matter of interest, of curiosity, or even it may be of suspicion, to consider what it is that we mean by the Classics; and conversely what it is that the Classics mean to us, and why we not merely invite but claim the active sympathy, the practical co-operation, alike of those whose primary interest lies in other fields of study, and of the whole body of our fellow-citizens. For our claim is made not only to those engaged in giving or receiving education, or in leading the life of scholars and students. It is made to the electorate of the whole nation; here in this city, to the 200,000 men and women on whom are laid the powers and the duties of citizenship, and all of whom, in some measure, share responsibility for the conduct of civic and national life on a fully civilised and fully humanised plane.

For education itself, and for many of its main factors, the names in use are casual and ill-defined. They are counters which pass insensibly through changes in value. But it is curious and significant that, with very few exceptions, they are of Greek or Latin origin. Education itself is a Latin word, of obscure etymology, and lending itself to different interpretations. Among the recognised subjects of education, it is only a small number of the simplest and most elementary that have English names: reading, writing, spelling, drawing, singing, and (this is neither accidental nor unsignifi-cant) games. Grammar, geography, history, arithmetic are Greek, literature and science are Latin words. So, too, with the faculties or schools of University studies. The faculties of arts, science, engineering, agriculture, medicine, com-merce are all called by Latin names and based on Roman or Graeco-Roman foundations. Those of music and theology are Greek. For the names

of educational organisations, the School, the
College, the University, we go back to the same
sources. All these facts are significant symbols.
They bring home the dependence of our civilisation on the roots from which it sprang and from
which it draws the sap of its life.

Two words in daily use, the one Latin, the
other Greek, have a special and a remarkable
history, the more worthy of notice because the
two studies they connote are the pivots on which
higher education is hung, or, to vary the metaphor,
the magnetic poles round which other studies
group and attach themselves, from which they
radiate. As instruments of training, as keys to
knowledge, as doors admitting to the whole world
of men and of things, they stand by themselves,
each unique and unreplaceable, and in their com-
bination of incalculable value. These are Classics
and Mathematics.

The Greek words *mathemata*, things learned,
and *mathematicé*, the art and craft of learning, had
already in the age of Plato come to take the meaning which they still bear ; things to be learned
primarily, necessarily, as a fundamental discipline
of the mind, and the substructure of all the natural
sciences and the productive industries. The Latin
words, Classics and Classical, are no less curious
in their history. " Classic" originally meant
simply "placed in a class." By an easy contraction of language, this came to mean "placed in a
high class," "first-class." The word *classicus* in
its earlier usage simply meant a scholar, one
proficient in the seven Liberal Arts so-called.
These were the acquirements or accomplishments
defined by Roman legislators as "worthy of a free

human being," *artes libero homine dignae;* they included both letters and science, and represented the sum of human or secular knowledge. Only about the time which we date by the death of Shakespeare and the birth of Milton do "the classical authors" begin to be spoken of with the implication or assumption, rather than any direct assertion, that they are the ancient Latin and Greek authors; it is about a century later, so it seems, before these authors received, at least in current usage, the short title of "the Classics," and later still before the term "Classical Studies" came into use to describe the studies which bear upon, or are accessible through, the languages in which these authors wrote, and the arts and civilisation of the world in which they lived. The older name for them, one no less magnificent in its claim, was "humane studies," *literae humaniores* or *artes humanitatis.*

If we wish, then, to use the name of the Classics as something more than a counter, as something expressing a real value, we must think of the Classics as those writings in which human language has been used to the best purpose and with the utmost perfection ; and of classical studies as the studies which interpret and are in turn interpreted by these writings. Or to put the same thing differently, we may find the warrant for calling anything a classic to which we find ourselves perpetually returning, and which we perpetually find, on returning to it, even greater than we thought. There are the modern as well as the ancient Classics. There are the Classics of Romanticism as well as those of the Graeco-Roman tradition. There are the Classics ot

England, of Italy, of France and Spain. Their
common quality is the attainment, in the vehicle
of language, of actual or approximate perfection; that perfection being, while of many kinds,
πολλῶν ὀνομάτων μορφὴ μία, the utmost attained
expression, in one way or another, of the spirit
of man.

On what grounds, then, is it justifiable to accept
the title in a specific or limited sense as meaning
the masterpieces of Greek and Latin literature?
Three may be named, all valid. First, the Greek
and Latin languages as developed by national and
individual genius are not only unsurpassed, but
in important respects unequalled, as vehicles of
human expression, alike in the power and the
delicacy of their mechanism. Secondly, expression has been given in them, once for all, to what
is primary and essential, whether in the record
and interpretation of history, in the field of thought
or speculation, in lessons for the conduct of life,
or in the creative achievements of poetry. Thirdly,
all that has come after them in Western Europe
or in the European worlds beyond the seas has
been built on their foundations, moulded by their
influence, saturated with their form and substance.
By losing touch with them, we cut ourselves off
from the sources of our civilisation, the anchorage
of our spirits, the sap of our life. It might even
be said that if, by some strange misfortune, we
had to make our choice between the Latin and
Greek Classics and the Classics of languages other
than Latin and Greek, it would be with the former
that we should find ourselves best armed and
equipped for understanding and dealing with life,
as well as introduced to the highest pleasures of

intellect and imagination. The Greek genius for asking the right question, the Roman faculty of finding the practical answer, apply to all the problems, whether analytic or constructive, with which we have to deal. But we have not to make any such choice. Both are before us. Both are, if we only want them enough, within our reach. And appreciation of our own English Classics is not diminished, it is more than doubled, by realising their descent from, their kinship with, those other Classics which we can likewise make our own.

In what sense, to what degree, can we make them our own? The case for the Greek and Latin Classics is often based on quite false grounds. A picture is drawn of the accomplished classical scholar, and people are asked to believe that this brilliant creature is the normal outcome of learning Greek and Latin. People do not believe it; nor could they, for it is patently untrue. The accomplished scholar, like the accomplished scientist or philosopher or artist, like the eminent statesman or the great captain of industry or the great Labour leader, is an exception, a rarity. What an attainable acquaintance with the Classics gives us is the power to appreciate and discriminate, to know the difference, or rather to feel it by a sort of instinct, between relevance and irrelevance, between accuracy and inaccuracy, between excellence and mediocrity. It gives what we most need, in the intellectual and artistic no less than the ethical and mechanical sphere, a standard.

This standard—at once an ideal kept in sight, a stimulus to effort, and a source of vitality—can only be secured by direct touch with work, whether ancient or modern, in which the standard is actually embodied. There are no short cuts to it, as there are no substitutes for it. There is no substitute for first-hand knowledge. But the virtue of the Classics is such, their vitalising power is so great, that a touch may be sufficient to create it. A chapter of prose, a dozen lines of poetry, if that prose or poetry be really classical—if, that is to say, it is the best, if it is of its kind perfect—can give a wholly new outlook, can admit into a larger and nobler world. Its effect may not be consciously realised at the time by the recipient; it need not be hammered in by the teacher; it cannot even be explained beforehand. It must be accepted in faith; time and experience will bring its verification.

It is not my business here—nor, I think I may say, even at the risk of misconception, is it the business of the Classical Association—to defend the Classics. In the statement of the objects of the Association the word "defence" does not occur. Its aim is to maintain and promote classical studies; and through these studies, to bring the Classics themselves more largely and more effectively into national life, to induce that contact with them which kindles imagination, quickens intelligence, and brings joy. We regard, or ought to regard, this contact with the Classics not as a thing to be fostered by artificial protection, not as a thing to be imposed by compulsion, but as a gift to be placed within reach, a privilege to be widely extended. Compulsory Greek and Latin are phrases as irrelevant as compulsory warmth and light. Such things are not compulsory, they are only necessary. But it is our business to endeavour that there shall be, so far as possible, no compulsory ignorance of them.

It is the contact which is essential. A touch may pass the current, may create the fertilisation. This is the sufficient answer to the objection that a little Latin or Greek is of no use. It is quality, not quantity, that matters. "The *Odyssey*," says Professor Whitehead, a little mournfully, in an admirable article on "The Place of the Classics in Education" in the *Hibbert Journal* for January last, "becomes insipid if you read it at the rate of five lines a day." The *Odyssey* need not be read at the rate of five lines a day, even by beginners; this is a point to which I shall return later. "*La jeunesse a du temps pour lire longuement, et de l'imagi-nation pour saisir toutes les grandes choses*": that is the saying not of a pedant or a dreamer or a theorist, but of Napoleon. It should be engraved on the hearts of all teachers.

But even taking the overstatement at its face value, do the objectors realise that even at that snail's progress the pupils, with their fresh intel-ligence, their young fearlessness, their potential imagination, would come on the seventh day to something that will revolutionise their whole out-look, will implant in them the germ of a new knowledge and power over life?

ὦ πόποι, οἶον δή νυ θεοὺς βροτοὶ αἰτιόωνται,
ἐξ ἡμέων γάρ φασι κάκ᾽ ἔμμεναι. οἱ δὲ καὶ αὐτοὶ
σφῇσιν ἀτασθαλίῃσιν ὑπὲρ μόρον ἄλγε᾽ ἔχουσιν.

Alas, how idly do these mortals blame
The Gods, as though by our devising came
The evils that, beyond what is ordained,
By their own folly for their grief they frame!

The three lines alone are, in the full sense of the words, a revelation, and a possession for ever. Or if the *Aeneid* be begun at the same snail's pace, it would be on the seventh day again that one would become possessed of the single line,

Tantae molis erat Romanam condere gentem,

which is the summing up of five hundred years of one of the most important phases—perhaps the most important phase—in human history. Contact with passages like these, the perfect crystallised expressions of human thought and human experience, is in fact more, not less valuable, because they reach us over a trajectory of two thousand or three thousand years, with the gathered momentum, the enriched associations, of their passage. Through them we can for a moment become, in the phrase of Plato, spectators of all time and of all existence ; and that moment will make a difference to us all the rest of our lives.

But the contact must be direct. To talk about the Classics—and that is just what, on an occasion like this, one feels acutely—is no substitute for letting the Classics themselves talk to one. The finest things that have been written about Homer or Plato, about Virgil or Horace, as about Milton or Wordsworth or Shakespeare, are but blurred and secondary impressions, often doing actual harm by interfering between the Classic itself and the intelligence and imagination that would spring of themselves to meet it. And from this law of direct contact it likewise follows that when the Classic is not in the mother-tongue, its place cannot be taken, its vital power cannot be communicated, by a translation. Translations of a Classic are at their

best only commentaries; of great use as helps,
but not substitutes. They may be, I am afraid
they often are, used, as Professor Whitehead says
in the article from which I have just quoted, "to
enable the pupil to get away from the Latin "—
or the Greek—"as quickly as possible, or to avoid
the stretch of mind in grappling with it." "Translation," said the German scholar Moritz Haupt,
"is the death of understanding." That is a hard
saying, but it states, with incisive force, what is
at least one side of a great truth. In education,
whether it be the education of childhood or of
later years, there is no substitute for first-hand
knowledge, no reservoir of surplus wealth to be
exploited: a capital levy cannot be made on learning; and you can only get ninepence for fourpence
by debasing the currency.

Shakespeare, in Jonson's well-known words,
"had small Latin and less Greek." There is no
harm in that; though the more the better. But
there is now a new danger, of which all who
appreciate the Classics in the larger as well as in
the more restricted sense of the term must be
conscious; and that is, to have no Latin and less
Greek.

Let me explain what I mean by an instance.
Some years ago there was published a volume of
what purported to be translations of Greek lyrical
poems. Among these was a little piece from the
Pseudo-Anacreontea which, in my schooldays (I
do not know whether it is so now), were much
used for beginners as being extremely simple. It
was the one beginning Οὔ μοι μέλει τὰ Γύγεω. The
translator rendered the words οὔ μοι μέλει, in all
good faith, "Do not sing to me." Now that is, in

itself, a trifle, a thing to raise a moment's amusement; but it is symptomatic of what is far from being a trifle. For this kind of misconception, based on an ignorance which does not even know that it is ignorant, can take effect in more important matters. It can distort to strange and perilous misuses such things as the psychology of Euripides or the passion of Sappho or the communism of Plato; it can vitiate the whole view of Greek thought and art and life.

There has been in recent years a great extension of interest and curiosity with regard to the Greek world. It has been stimulated by the wonderful discoveries of archaeology, by the application to historical study of new and powerful methods, and by the popularisation of the Attic drama and of the political and social theories or doctrines of Greek thinkers. The spectacle of Greek life has been filmed, as one might say, for a large popular audience. But the cinema, however high its cultural value may be estimated, can hardly be called a severe intellectual discipline, and the pictures of life it presents do not always bear much relation to reality. And so it is that there are considerable numbers of people who know less than no Greek. Something has reached them which derives from Greece, but has become diluted or distorted or debased in transmission. It may retain enough of its virtue to act, but to act, according to the circumstances, as an intoxicant, or a narcotic, or a high-explosive. Against this real danger, the touch of the Greek Classics themselves is the protection; for they, like all Classics, and eminently so because their quality is quite unique and incomparable, have not only a stimulating but a steadying, not only a kindling but an illuminating power.

"Nothing," as Arnold says, "has a right to be satisfied with itself, to be and remain itself, except that which has reached perfection; nothing has the right to impose itself on the rest of the world except that which is of higher perfection than the rest of the world." That is, in one sentence, the case for the Classics. It is a great claim to make. It is made not for Greek as such, nor for Latin as such, but for the Classics as such; for the records, that is to say, in which at any time, in any country and language, the spirit of man has expressed itself most perfectly. It is a claim, on their behalf and on ours, for what an English Classic, who was also Member of Parliament for Bristol, Burke, nobly called "a partnership in all perfection." And it rests its particular application on the fact, alike important and indisputable, that the perfection of the Greek and Latin Classics is the highest; that they give us, more than others, a standard of appreciation, a sense of basic values, a clear vision of life and a corresponding increase in the power of handling it. To become partners in that perfection, we must know what it means; and we can only know what anything means by knowing the thing itself. We can only know what the Greek perfection means by knowing Greek, by seeing with our eyes and handling with our hands (if I may dare without irreverence to apply words so sacred) that which was from the beginning, the word of life.

The Classics have an eternal power of disengaging themselves, alike from the oblivion of neglect and from the accretions and superstructures of their commentators. They are analysed, pulled to pieces, quarried for subsidiary purposes. They are often mishandled and misinterpreted. They may become overlaid by absorption in the ancillary studies—archaeology, grammar, primitive religion, textual criticism, and a hundred others, all in their place useful or necessary or interesting—which group themselves round the central object, appreciation of the Classics themselves. When the dust settles, they are there as before, in their high station, in their quiet beauty, in their quickening power.

One of my predecessors took for the subject of his address to the Association (an address which no one who heard it will have forgotten) "A Scholar's Religion," *Religio Grammatici.* Religion comes to us not only as a word from the Latin language, but largely also as a thing from the Latin character. "Religio" was a study and a practice ; the reading over and over, the com- mitting to heart—or, more deeply, the taking to heart—of the lessons of sound doctrine in form and substance. It may stray away into what was in Latin called "superstitio," into devotion paid to the extraneous, the unessential. It is in this sense that classical studies may become, what they are often undiscriminatingly called, a superstition. But work is no superstition ; and I should like to say a word here to teachers of the Classics. Most of your work, as of every one's work in this world, is routine. It would be idle to say that it is always pleasant, or that it is habitually inspiring. Inspiration must be brought to your work ; it does not come from your work. More even for you, therefore, than for others is it necessary

o

to have that vital touch with the Classics which
gives you the consciousness that your work, if
it be only that of a stoker in the furnaces, of a
bricklayer or mortar-mixer for the house of
wisdom, is your contribution to the partnership
in all perfection.

The celebrated words of Newman in *The
Grammar of Assent* are almost too well known
to quote ; yet I may be allowed to quote them,
because, written as they are about the Classics,
they have themselves the classic quality of which
they give so accurate and so beautiful a description.    He has just mentioned Homer and Horace
as representative Classics.

" Passages which to a boy are but rhetorical
commonplaces, neither better nor worse than a
hundred others which any clever writer might
supply, which he gets by heart, and thinks
very fine, and imitates as he thinks successfully, at length come home to him when long
years have passed, and he has had experience
of life, and pierce him as if he had never
before known them, with their sad earnestness
and vivid exactness.    Then he comes to understand how it is that lines, the birth of some
chance morning or evening at an Ionian festival
or among the Sabine hills, have lasted generation
after generation, for thousands of years, with a
power over the mind, and a charm, which the
current literature of his own day, with all its
obvious advantages, is utterly unable to rival."

*They come home to him, and pierce him as if he
had never before known them*—this is what the
Classics, in the true sense of the word "classic,"
do.    This is their central and lasting value.    It is

the same thing which was put in words equally memorable by Shelley in his definition or explanation of poetry, that "it makes familiar objects be as if they were not familiar"; not by wrapping the objects in a mist, not by distorting or falsifying them, but by lifting a veil from off them, by revealing them in their actual truth. To have attained this vision is to have overcome the world. What we aim at is that the chance, or something more than the chance, of obtaining it should be extended largely, the way made plain for it, the labour required for reaching it insisted on, guided, stimulated. Success in that effort stands between us and a tragedy, that the equality towards which the world is consciously tending may be a low and not a high equality. To be in touch with the Classics, let me repeat once more, for it is the conclusion of the whole matter, is to be in touch with the highest; it is to have a standard of perfection, and not to be satisfied with less. Fall short of it doubtless we must. But if we aim low, we shall never reach high.

The two Classics named by Newman in the passage I quoted, Homer in Greek, Horace in Latin, are aptly chosen: for Homer is at the source, Horace at the last culmination, of the world which contained Greece and Rome. Let me ask you to pause on them for a moment, not to dilate on their excellences—that would be needless—not to weigh them against other Classics— that would be futile—but to realise how nearly they are both within our reach.

It has been said, and there is truth in the saying, that Plato and Aristotle are the great permanent argument for Greek: Aristotle as the founder of organised science, the creator of logic, the analyst of human life in the individual and the community ; Plato as the most daring, subtle, and profound of thinkers. But they are difficult; they demand mature intelligence and a large measure of trained scholarship. Or again, Herodotus and Thucydides are the foundation-stones for the whole study and understanding of history; but they have to be read and known as wholes in order to make their effect. Homer is different. Not all, not perhaps very many, yet many more than one may think, can even begin to learn Greek. But all who begin to learn Greek can begin to read and to enjoy Homer, can make direct contact with the earliest and greatest of poets, the fountain-head not only of Greek but of Latin and English poetry. Let me cite what is being done at this moment in a London Secondary School, where two-thirds of the pupils come from Elementary Schools, and where a few years ago no Greek was taught at all. " My Greek beginners, in their second term, are reading Homer and enjoying it immensely. They have done over three hundred lines in about a fortnight, and are getting right into it now." That, you will notice, is something different from five lines a day. But this is not all. Greek is already in that school a coveted privilege. " A whole Latin division are now clamouring to be allowed to begin Greek."

This, it may be said, is due to the energy and enthusiasm of an exceptional teacher. No doubt it is. What we require is that such energy and enthusiasm should not be exceptional. But I had rather say that it was due to the teacher's belief in the Classics. With that belief, the mountains that are said to stand in the way—the prejudice of parents, the tyranny of examinations, the apathy or hostility of educational authorities—will turn into mice. "We know our own affairs," as Mr. Lockit observes to his daughter Lucy, "therefore let us have no more whimpering or whining." But "schoolmasters and schoolmistresses," as was pathetically said to me the other day, "are human, and like to have something or some one else to blame, whether it is the examination system, or the Universities, or the Local Education Authority, or the Board of Education."

ἐξ ἡμέων γάρ φασι κάκ' ἔμμεναι· οἱ δὲ καὶ αὐτοὶ
σφῇσιν ἀτασθαλίῃσιν ὑπὲρ μόρον ἄλγε' ἔχουσιν.

The Classics, be they Greek or Latin or English, leave us all, as they found us, exceedingly human. But the vitality that we can draw from them ought to give us, does give us except by our own fault, power as well as intelligence, courage as well as insight. Timidity means incompetence; a merely defensive attitude means paralysis.

Or again, take Horace. Here the case is even clearer. For in the first place, such knowledge of Latin as allows of the *Odes* being read with intelligence and a good deal of appreciation is well within the reach of the ordinary schoolboy or schoolgirl who leaves school at sixteen ; and in the second place, Horace is emphatically one of those Classics who are of no use at all except in the original. In translation, or even in loose paraphrase, Homer remains interesting and exciting : nothing, in particular, can spoil the *Odyssey* or make it cease to be the best story in the world. But the virtue of Horace is untransferable. All translations of him are vapid, most are painfully or ludicrously so. It is he himself alone who is—who may be even for those who know but little Latin—not merely an artist in language but a master in life; one whose own central outlook on life and grasp over it may be widely caught and shared, and will tell far more and more as years bring experience. Among the world Classics, or even among the Latin Classics alone, others are greater, others soar to higher heights and plumb deeper depths; but he is at the centre. He touches us with an intimacy that nearly two thousand years seem only to have drawn closer, with a sustaining and illuminating power that is the more potent because it works so quietly and almost insensibly.

Seven years ago, reference was made in a brilliant Defence of Classical Education to "misconceptions prevalent"—I quote the author's words—among "business men in Leeds or Bristol, who have never had occasion to think at all deeply." I know of no business man, in Bristol or elsewhere, who in these times, whether he thinks deeply or not, has not plenty of occasion to do so. Now, the Classics, if they are properly used (and they cannot be used unless they are known) make us think more deeply by bringing us alongside of the deepest human thought. And of this there is a growing sense, both among employers and employed, in the world of commerce and industry. "Business," the late George Wyndham wrote to a friend when Under-Secretary of State for War at a time of high pressure and great anxiety, "is a capital exercise. It gives you a number of occasions every day for doing the right thing in the right way." That is exact truth ; and the Classics are a standard and example of right things done in the right way. With the doing of wrong things in the right way we are familiar ; it is what is known as the doctrine of efficiency. Whether, or how far, it is possible to do right things in the wrong way is a question which I may content myself with commending to your consideration. At all events it is not desirable. And no less suggestive are the words in which the letter continues : " but I do not believe that the second-class clerks could work as they do if we had not all the abstract speculation of three thousand years behind us."

Classical scholars are accused of exaggerating, as no doubt all specialists are apt to do, the importance of their own special studies ; and classical studies may be so pursued as to justify the accusation. What I wish to do is to impress the point that they can and should be pursued otherwise. To the Classics in their true sense, to the masterpieces of human language recording and giving voice to the highest efforts or achievements of the human soul, the importance attached is far more likely to be too little than too much. To have known the best, and to have known it for the best, is success in life.

There are other tasks and duties, other interests and occupations. Some, even many, of these may be closer or larger, may have prior or superior claims. I need not waste time by speaking of the evils of over-specialisation. Yet to any one who urges this in a spirit of impatience, I might reply in the words of Gambetta, " *Qui donc entends-je parler de la République universelle ? N'avons nous pas assez de peine à fonder notre République à nous ?* "

This "republic of our own," the commonwealth of the classics, is our first concern as a Classical Association. And the inspiration which the Classics give extends far beyond the sphere of letters. Courage and faith will not limit themselves. Truth and beauty once known are known once for all.

To those of my colleagues, if there be any, who are downhearted, let me recall the answer made by the hero of the *Odyssey*, when Telemachus has counted up the overwhelming number of their opponents and asked despairingly whom they can find to help them :

> τοιγὰρ ἐγὼν ἐρέω, σὺ δὲ σύνθεο καί μευ ἄκουσον
> καὶ φράσαι ἤ κεν νῶιν 'Αθήνη σὺν Διί πατρὶ
> ἄρκεσει, ἠέ τιν' ἄλλον ἀμύντορα μερμηρίξω ;

and the rejoinder of Telemachus :

> ἐσθλώ τοι τούτω γ' ἐπαμύντορε τοὺς ἀγορεύεις
> ὕψι περ' ἐν νεφέεσσι καθημένω, ὤ τε καὶ ἄλλοις
> ἀνδράσι τε κρατέουσι καὶ ἀθανάτοισι θεοῖσιν.

"Surely I will tell you; do you mark, and listen to me, and say whether for you and me Athena with Zeus her father will suffice, or shall I cast about for some other helper ? "

"Good helpers are those two whom you name, high though they sit among the clouds, for they have power over all men and over the Gods that do not die."

Let that be one of the messages for us of the Greek Classics. And as complementary to it, take a Latin prayer, not from Horace, but a prayer that Horace heard made, on the night of the

31st May, 17 B.C., *in campo ad Tiberim*, and see whether we do not gather from it a flash of the Roman temper and the Roman devotion.

It is preserved in the fragments of the *Acta Secularia*, discovered in Rome little more than thirty years ago. These were the official record, engraved on slabs of marble, of the ceremonies at the celebration of the Secular games by Augustus and the re-consecration, as one may say, of Rome under the Peace of the Empire. It is in this record that one comes, with a strange thrill, on the terse entry *Carmen composuit Quintus Horatius Flaccus*. But it is not the familiar words of the Secular Hymn which I quote; it is the prayer offered by the Emperor to the Moerae, the *Fata Deum*, the Powers who sway heaven and earth, for the Commonwealth. Than these words we shall find no nobler expression of aspiration, whether for the Empire to which we belong or for *notre République à nous*, the Commonwealth of learning and of the arts of civilisation.

"Vos quaeso precorque uti imperium maiestatemque Populi Romani Quiritium duelli domique auxitis utique semper Latinum nomen tueamini, incolumitatem sempiternam victoriam valetudinem Populo Romano Quiritibus tribuatis remque publicam Populi Romani Quiritium salvam servetis."

I will not insult the majesty of the Latin or the intelligence of the audience by offering a translation. The words are more than a formula of ritual; they have the great classic quality : weight of meaning, direct simplicity, depth of controlled emotion, lucid completeness, and unadorned magnificence ; and with these, the special Latin gift, the *imperatoria brevitas* in which Rome set a model for the admiration and despair of mankind.  In brevity at least one may attempt to follow their example; and on this prayer I will end; but with one final word from an English Classic, to remind us not only of the splendour of "the immaterial ideal of spiritual and intellectual perfection," but of the labour through which it must be sought, the arduousness of ascent that has to be set against it, the joy of effort and the triumph of increasing accomplishment: "the arduous ladder whereby man climbs towards his perfection, towards that unattainable but irresistible lodestar, gazed after with earnest longing and invoked with bitter tears, the longing of thousands of hearts, the tears of many generations."

# XI

## THE PLACE OF THE CLASSICS IN IMPERIAL STUDIES

An Address delivered at the Midland Institute, Birmingham, February 23, 1925.

In the choice of this subject for an address to your Institute, I have followed what I believe to be the admirable tradition which it has followed for the half-century and more of its existence, that of placing before its members, and before the large public, matters not of local and temporary interest only, but those which have a wider bearing, whether in the sphere of science and industry, of letters and art, or of political and social organisation. That the Classics have a high and peculiar value, a function which should be recognised and secured in the life not only of the city or the nation but of the Empire, is the claim which I ask you to consider, and the conclusion for which I hope to gain—or may I rather say, to confirm ?—your acceptance.

Nowhere can such a claim be urged more suitably than in this great centre of English life, linked as it is through its industries and commerce with all the British Dominions, prominent as it stands in the development of civic institutions, in the organisation of national education, and in the number of distinguished citizens, past and present, whose influence and example have extended beyond the city itself and beyond the area of which it may be called the capital, to the furthest quarters of the world.

There is a well-known story of Sir Walter Scott, in half-humorous resentment at a depreciating remark made about his countrymen by Bolton, the great Birmingham engineer, "In every corner of the world you will find a Scot and a rat," having retorted, "and a Brummagem button": to which Bolton rejoined, "We make something better in Birmingham than buttons; we make power." It is almost exactly one hundred years ago that Scott acknowledged the justice of Bolton's vindication of his native town, in paying an eloquent tribute to those "whose genius invents and executes those wonderful combinations which extend in such an incalculable degree the human force and command over the physical world." But now, as then and at all times, the power which genius exercises, the combinations which it calls into being, are not only or even mainly mechanical; they are intellectual and moral. The disciplined intelligence; the grasp of history; the sense of the continuity of civilisation; the faculty of clear thinking and of exact expression of thought; commerce with the greatest minds and appreciation of their achievements: these are what give power and enable its effective use.

It will be within the recollection of some, probably of a good many here, that last May there was held in the British Empire Exhibition at Wembley, in such time as could be salvaged from the more material or more strictly exhibitional sides of its vast programme, an Educational Conference at which the doctrine of Imperial Studies was promulgated, and papers were read and discussions held on the various sides from which Imperial Education may be approached, and on the methods for developing and organising it. I will not say that this Conference attracted eager crowds, or that it depleted either the Machine Galleries or the Amusements Park; but it did useful work. Stress was naturally laid on those studies and those subjects which bear directly and obviously on what the British Empire is, how it grew up, how it is managed, what it stands for to all the kingdoms and dominions and dependencies which make up a great and as yet incompletely realised and only partially integrated Commonwealth of Nations. Special emphasis was given to the teaching of the history of the Empire in all our schools; to the close association of that history with geography; and to the inter-connection of these, not only with one another, but with instruction, from the Elementary School upwards, in the mechanism of industry and commerce, in the articulation of the social fabric and in the principles of citizenship. Emphasis was also, and with no less justice, laid on the fact, one never to be lost sight of, that no intelligent grasp of the Empire as it is can be gained without some understanding of the processes through which it came into being and the roots from which it sprang; and further, that the duties of citizenship —whether that be the local citizenship of a community or the national citizenship of our country or the wider Imperial citizenship which we are beginning to realise and helping or hindering (the former, it may be hoped) to construct, or even, though this goes beyond my immediate scope, the ultimate citizenship of the world—that these duties and the responsibilities attaching to them involve, for their performance and discharge, foundations solidly based on consciousness of the past; and that only thus can we deal intelligently and effectively with the problems of the present, only thus frame the fabric, and work towards the realisation, of a nobler future.

For all these as for all other studies, language is the common, universal, and necessary vehicle. And language put to its best purpose, used at its utmost power and with the greatest skill, and recorded that it may not pass away, evaporate and be forgotten, is what we call, for want of a better word, literature. Of that word I am not particularly fond. It is much misused, and often carries with it the notion of something artificial and apart from life. William Morris once called it "a beastly French word." It is, of course, not French any more than it is English or Italian or, for the matter of that, German. It is a Latin word, invented as a translation of the Greek word *grammaticé*, instruction in letters beginning with the alphabet. But afterwards it took quite a different meaning; it was a quality, or a possession, of what we should call educated persons. Their literature meant their acquaintance with letters, with the records of human thought and experience set down in books. According to the measure and extent of his literature, of the amount and quality of that acquaintance, a man was, more or less, literate. Without some amount of it at the least, he was illiterate. This latter word we still use, much in its original meaning.

What I have just said is a digression, but it is not irrelevant to the subject we are exploring: for it gives an instance, one out of a thousand, of the advantage of studying language closely and using it precisely. Whether or how far we can think except in words is a problem which may be left to the psychologists; what is certain is, that our thought cannot be much in advance of our power of expressing it, and that if it cannot be clearly expressed, that means that it is not clear itself. And our power of communicating thought, our power of explanation or persuasion, depends entirely on our power of expression.

It is only, then, through language, and through literature in its wider and truer sense, that Imperial Studies, be they what they may, can be pursued. It is only through them that the sense of community can be established beyond the very limited sphere of what the individual, in a very short life and with but small first-hand experience, can attain. They are, in the fine phrase of Keats, the openers of the doors leading to universal knowledge.

While, then, at the Wembley Conference it was education in the history and geography, the commerce and industries, the political, economic, and social organisation of the Empire that occupied the foreground, some stress was also laid, though rather incidentally, on language and literature, as elements in Imperial Education. They were not ignored. But literature was chiefly touched on as an adjunct to or an ornament of these other studies; and language was hardly touched on at all. Further, in this part of the field, it was the

English language and what has been or is being written in English to which reference was practically confined. The Classics were not even mentioned.

Now, English is the mother-tongue not of England only, but, broadly and largely speaking, of the Empire. Of course this can only be said with large exceptions or qualifications. Apart from the vast extent and the numerical preponderance of the Asiatic and African races, with their own languages and some of them with their own important literatures, other European languages have to be taken into the account. Within Great Britain there is the Welsh of Wales, and to a less but a quite considerable extent the Gaelic of North-Western Scotland. There is the Erse of Ireland; the French of Lower Canada; the Dutch of South Africa; the Spanish of British Honduras; and others elsewhere. But it remains true that English already is, and tends more and more to be, the common Imperial language; and that it is books or newspapers written in English which the citizens of the Empire throughout its dominions in both hemispheres read now, and will continue to read. Obviously, then, it was natural that English should not be largely discussed as a subject of Imperial study, simply because it was taken for granted. It was taken for granted, too, that any work of real value, whether in history or science or economics or poetry or what not, brought out in English in any part of the Empire would find its audience there and could also find its way to the other parts of the Empire by natural process.

For somewhat different reasons, little or nothing,

I think, was said about the claims of other modern European languages to be recognised as having in some measure a place of their own in Imperial Studies. The British Empire and the English-speaking nations are connected to these other nations and tongues by a thousand ties of past history and of actual relationships, political, commercial, social, and intellectual. The union or federation of Commonwealths which we call the Empire is, in a wider view, only one part of a greater world-union; the civilisation of the Empire is but part, though for us the part of far the greatest and most immediate importance, of civilisation itself. And so we find, for instance, that without any express regulation, still less any compulsion, French is part of the course of instruction in all, or practically all, Secondary Schools, not in England alone but in many of the Dominions.

Latin and Greek are on a different footing. The claim they have to be ranked among Imperial Studies rests on different grounds. This is the claim which I invite you to consider.

But first, let us distinguish. The title chosen for this lecture is, as you will have noticed, not "The Place of Greek and Latin," but "The Place of the Classics" in Imperial Studies. The distinction is important. Of the value of Latin and Greek as languages merely, as instruments of intellectual discipline, as an exercise or drill for the mind much as certain physical exercises are for the body, it would be easy to speak, and I could, if necessary, say a good deal about it. It is because, as languages, they are mechanisms of incomparable precision and finish, that they have such a high value—higher in this respect than the value of

P

any modern language—in making the mind into a competent instrument for doing its job, whatever that may be. But that is not my point. It does not bear on Imperial Studies as such. It only means that, in all education alike, certain subjects, of which this is one, have a special disciplinary value, a special stimulating or strengthening power towards training the mind. It is less a matter of Imperial concern than of mere common sense, that in education we should use the best implements as well as the best methods. Which are the best implements, or the best available—it is our business, of course, to see to it that the best are made available—is a matter on which there will always be, and will quite reasonably be, large difference of opinion, large and useful variation in practice. As to some, there would be unanimity ; as to others, only a preponderance of assent and a distinct divergence of opinion. But this, as I said, is not my point. Neither arithmetic, nor French, nor Latin, to take instances of the three kinds, is, as such, an Imperial study.

Nor is it my point to urge another argument sometimes advanced, that "one of the ways of teaching people to write good English is to teach them Greek or Latin." No doubt it is; and no doubt the mastery of good English—in other words, the power of expressing one's meaning simply, clearly, and gracefully—is what should be cultivated throughout a civilised English-speaking empire. But the claim I urge for inclusion in Imperial Studies is not made for the Latin and Greek languages. It is made for the Classics—for the knowledge and study of these masterpieces in which the human spirit reached, more nearly than before or since, towards perfection ; which are the embodiment or record of the deepest and truest thought, the highest ideals and aspirations, the most instructive and most remarkable achievements of mankind.

On the Graeco-Roman civilisation of which these Classics are the legacy, our own civilisation is founded. From it, as a matter not of argumentative theory but of plain historical fact, we derive our institutions, our ways of life, our methods of thinking and acting. In our world, to quote a famous and familiar saying, nothing moves that is not derived from Greece, nothing stands that is not derived from Rome. Mother-country and Dominions alike share this common parentage. Ill for them it would be if they forgot it. Forgotten or not, the community of ancestry lives in our blood. But we can let it live in us consciously and actively. The Classics are not dead ancestors, to whose graves we may go for sentimental interest or for idle amusement or for the payment of conventional and formulary rites. They are alive, not merely in us dimly and unconsciously through long transmission, but for us directly and vitally, if we are given the opportunity, and will take the pains, to learn their language, to understand their message, to incorporate them into our own thought and life.

It is very essential to realise, and it is not generally realised enough, how much, whether in a nation or in an empire, community—the sense of common aims and pursuits and interests, of mutual understanding and mutual goodwill, is based, in fact, on a common historic past, in feeling, on the consciousness of that past. I may be allowed to touch briefly on both aspects of the case as they bear on the subject we are considering.

Greece and Rome between them organised life, made man for the first time fully human and fully civilised. The Greek genius, with its lucidity, its fearlessness, its searching directness, laid out the ground-plan on which all succeeding ages have worked. The Latin genius, constructive rather than creative, did something different but perhaps as great; it built the framework of the structure which we, and those to come after us, have for our task to amplify, to complete, to adapt to changing conditions. It made an empire based on citizenship. It set up and transmitted a pattern which repays the closest study, an example which we have indeed to vary and expand and modify largely, but which on its broad lines we have not yet bettered, and may be well pleased if we can equal.

The whole of our thought and theory on political and social matters comes from Greece, be it Conservatism or Liberalism or Socialism or what you will. To grasp the principles of all or any of these fully and clearly, we—by we, I mean the educated citizens of the Empire—must know Greek. I do not mean that all of us either must or can. Nor do I make the absurd claim that knowledge of Greek necessarily gives this understanding. The claim I do make is that towards having it, knowledge of the Greek classics is an all but indispensable condition; and that towards having it effectively, that knowledge must be, as largely as possible, first-hand. Much may be learned from reading modern histories of Greece. Much may be learned, at least by those of peculiar intelligence and aptitude, from reading English translations of the Greek Classics, the greatest observers and thinkers of the world, Thucydides, let us say, or Plato, or Aristotle. But in this way we can, unless we are exceptionally gifted, only get at their meaning as dimmed or distorted, to a greater or less degree but to a large degree at the best, by a refracting or opaque medium. To any one who doubts this, it is only necessary to point out that, from generation to generation, Greek history is being perpetually rewritten, and the Greek Classics are being perpetually retranslated. Both are make-shift work. If we had nothing to go upon now but the histories and translations of one hundred years ago, or even fifty years ago, we should have already lost touch with this element in our spiritual ancestry. The same thing would be happening as happened to Western Europe in the Middle Ages when Greek was lost to it. The rediscovery of Greek at the Renaissance gave the intellectual impulse which created the modern world. But it took generations of hard work to master again what had been forgotten; in fact, the process of recovery is still going on. If we lost Greek again, our successors, generations hence, would have to rediscover it anew. Therefore, while knowledge of Greek must probably always be confined to a comparatively small number of people, it should be as widely spread as possible; and ample pro-vision for its being learned, and for the training of men and women competent to teach it, is a matter of high national and high Imperial concern.

What I have said about Greek as giving the origin of all our thought and theory applies in main substance to Latin as being the basis of all our life and practice. But there are two important distinctions to be noted: first, that Latin lies behind not English only but the other European languages as well, as a sort of second mother-tongue; that the framework of European speech, the construction of European writing, are directly based on the Latin which was for ages, and up to quite recent times, the common or international language of all educated people; and secondly, that the European conception of civilised life which is the motive force of nation and Empire alike is built up on Latin foundations.

It is worth while looking into this latter point more closely as it concerns Imperial Studies and the life of the Empire.

Greece, the body of the Greek Classics, contains all our germinal ideas; it is an inexhaustible inspiration. But Greek history is the history of one long failure to create and establish an empire, that is to say, an organic Commonwealth of States or Nations. Hellenism was a common spirit: it meant, or ought to have meant—many of their best thinkers and statesmen felt this fully and said this clearly—Hellenic unity. But that was never effected. Sectionalism—not so much the modern sectionalism of one class or interest against another as the conflict of one civic unit against another—defeated all efforts towards the realisation of a Greek Commonwealth. Within the civic unit many of the greatest achievements of mankind were made. An unequalled intensity and brilliance of life were reached. Social experiments were made with a hardihood, a merciless logical completeness, only possible perhaps on that small scale, where a recalcitrant minority could be (and

often was) expelled bodily and driven into exile.
But even between tyrannies or oligarchies or
democracies the bond of union was very frail;
and the colonies sent out from Athens or Corinth
or Miletus into this Greater Greece beyond the
seas left them for good like a swarm out of a hive:
often relations between them and the mother-
cities became those of jealous and bitter hostility.
There were vague attempts at union.   There was
an Amphictyonic Council, a body of delegates from
the Greek States, which might have developed
into something like our own Imperial Conferences,
or even into a sort of League of Nations.   It never
came to anything.   There were the Panhellenic
festivals, the famous Olympian games pre-eminent
among them, which drew together not only the
athletes but the artists and men of letters from all
parts of the Greek world.   There was free inter-
communication of preachers, philosophers, artists,
men of science.   There was some general sense
of common Hellenism as against the non-Hellenic
or barbarian world.   This was often appealed to.
But even under the terror of the Persian invasion
the appeal only took effect partially; and it never
afterwards took effect at all.   Even peace between
Greek States was made for fixed periods only.
There was perpetual regrouping of transitory
alliances.   Thus the life of Greece wasted away
in internecine conflict.   As soon as a solid military
power was organised in Macedonia, Greece
collapsed, as Herodotus had foreseen, a century
before it happened, would be the result of any
Great Power establishing itself in the Balkan
Peninsula.   The Greek genius, acute, splendid,
and searching, was not practical; it could not

realise, still less work steadily towards, any larger development.

That was the task and the accomplishment of Rome. One is sometimes reminded of the two architects who, as the story went, had had to make their claims in competition before a public meeting at Athens. The one gave an able and eloquent discourse on the principles of architecture and their application. When he had finished, the other got up and said, "What this man has said to you, I can do " : and he got the contract.

Step by step, slowly, patiently, and inflexibly, the constructive Latin genius, backed by the disciplined power of Rome, spread throughout the Mediterranean world first the aim, then the accomplished fact, of a single and inclusive Imperial citizenship. It established and secured the freedom of the seas. Its roads, by land no less than by sea, made communication easy and commerce ubiquitous. The Latin colonies planted in the provinces were each a centre for the Romanisation of the whole surrounding district. There was a unified code of Imperial law, with a central Court of final appeal. There was interimperial free trade. There was a centralised Government recruited in its personnel from the whole Empire without distinction of race or birth, which fostered and guided the municipalisation of local life in self-governing civic communities. There was an Imperial army and navy alongside of and behind the local and provincial forces. There was even what might be called a common Imperial religion symbolised in the worship paid to the Genius of the Emperor as head or chief servant of the Commonwealth.

This achievement of Rome is a permanent lesson for mankind. It is one of continual and even of increasing value. It is one which we as the inheritors, as the maintainers, and even in our degree as constructors of an Empire in its largest, most beneficent and most exalted meaning, cannot afford to neglect. We cannot, therefore, afford to neglect the studies through which it is known, and the great classical writers in whom s spirit is embodied most fully.

But while this is true as regards the successes of Rome in that great human task, it is no less true as regards Rome's failures; the flaws, the weaknesses, the false steps and miscalculations which were in the structure of the fabric, and which led to its decay and at last to its collapse. From these we have lessons to learn of equal importance. History, it is true, does not repeat itself; but the lessons of history bear, and demand, perpetual repetition. To pursue this into detail would take long and would be beyond our present scope. But we may note in passing, though even this is a digression, some causes of disintegration which are, among others, borne in upon us by study of the Latin Classics.

There was aggregation into huge cities, due to the real comforts as well as the superficial attractions of urban life ; and with that, rural depopulation and reliance on foreign sources for food supplies.

There was a vicious fiscal system arising out of defective theories of economics which clogged up the sources of wealth. Under it, the incidence of taxation was such as to crush the middle class out between the profiteers and the proletariat.

There was more and more dilution of the pure
Latin stock, itself inadequate in numbers for the
burden laid upon it.

There were ravages of epidemics of a malarial
type previously unknown, which not only killed
off enormous numbers, but seem to have permanently enfeebled the survivors for several
generations.

With the increasing complexity of the Govern-
mental machine, as it took more and more control,
there was a weakening sense of patriotism and
loss of the instinct for self-government. The
State, that is to say, the bureaucracy, had to do
everything.

More largely, there was a mysterious loss of
intellectual and moral fibre. Betting and gambling
were almost universal. Indecent novels and
spiritualistic treatises, we are informed, almost
killed serious reading, so that the great public
libraries were neglected or even closed. And on
the top of all this a spirit of apathy and hope-
lessness grew. The thing is put in these words
by a Latin writer, not, indeed, one of the Classics,
but recalling here the classical touch by the weight
and brevity of his expression, " mundus iam
senescit." " By this we know that the earth falls
asunder, being old."

One problem, indeed, we have to face and con-
quer which was absent in both the Greek and the
Latin world, though from very different reasons;
that is, friction and clash of interests between
self-governing, proud, largely independent communities within the Empire. This did not occur
in Greece because, as I have noted, there was no
Empire within which it could occur. The com-

plete independence, the autonomy as they called it, of each city-state was all-powerful. It submitted with great reluctance even to the loose bond of a league; that it should yield so far as to allow of coalescence in a larger organism was a thing beyohd all range of possibility. The intellectual and artistic commonwealth they realised; there they stopped. The result was that Greece dwindled into a province first of the Macedonian, then of the Roman Empire.

Rome, on the other hand, steadily pursued the object of welding all her dominions into a single fabric; leaving the existing municipal or cantonal systems as far as possible alone, encouraging them to frame themselves more and more on Latin models, and supplying them with revised constitutions, but deprecating, guarding against, and even on occasion forcibly repressing the growth of separatist national feeling. The countries over which Roman rule was gradually and often very reluctantly extended were divided administratively into provinces. They were not, they were not meant to be, and they seldom even desired to be, states or nations in any real sense. First individuals, then separate towns or communities, finally the whole of the provincial populations, were gradually admitted into full citizenship. But this was the Roman or Imperial citizenship. There were provincial assemblies, of a rather ornamental kind, though sometimes they had large functions and fostered a sense of provincial unity. But it was not until the fabric of empire had become loosened and begun to fall asunder that there was any movement towards national separation, or the creation of distinct states within the Empire.

Even these slight sketches of a vast field may indicate how much may be drawn from a study of the Graeco-Latin world, in warning or example, in stimulus towards constructive action and in grasp of the movement of civilisation, both in these respects and in others on which it would be easy to dilate; and may induce you to realise that such study is matter of Imperial concern.

Now I need not labour the point to which these considerations lead up. It is this. In order that such study may be fruitfully pursued, a foundation must be laid by large provision, in England, and not in England only but throughout all the Dominions, for study of the Greek and Latin languages. There is already in this country, there is also in the Australian Commonwealth, a distinct and hopeful revival of that study; and not only a revival, but a revivification. It is pursued by improved methods, with more intelligence and more interest. This growth should be recognised and fostered. It will enrich public as well as individual life. It will add future strength to the bonds of union among the nations which constitute the British Commonwealth by giving consciousness of the common foundations on which they are built, the roots, deep in the past, from which they have drawn their life. It will establish the sense of kinship in a common spiritual ancestry. That sense of kinship goes far, indeed is invaluable, towards giving common ground and establishing mutual understanding.

Now, in this sphere, just as much as in the sphere of the material world, we cannot go on for long living on capital. Wealth is in both the daily creation of daily labour. Or, to vary the

metaphor, it is only by unceasing cultivation that
fertility can be ensured and continuance of crops
kept up. Learning is not a thing that can be
banked, that can be deposited in a museum to be
looked up on holidays, or be put away in cold
storage, to be drawn upon when occasion arises.
It is a vital energy. "Men die, and with them
goes the bulk of what they had learned during
their lives; we want an unceasing succession."
The study of which I have been speaking must
be constantly provided for and pursued.

"We all of us spend half of our time in misunderstanding our neighbours." That misunderstanding, which is so disastrous, means that we
really talk in different languages; that we use
words in different senses, or in no clear sense at
all. If any one asks here, like the lawyer in the
Gospel, "Who is my neighbour?" the answer for
my present purpose is, "Every fellow-citizen of
the Empire." Dangerous as such misunderstanding is in ordinary intercourse and in smaller
communities, it is more dangerous, because less
easily corrected, between the members of a world-
wide confederation. It has been said, and I think
with much truth, that the only real peril to
friendly relations between Great Britain and the
United States is that both nations think they are
using the same language when they really are
not, and use different language when they mean
the same thing. This applies within the bounds
of our own Empire also. Against that risk, the
common basis of knowledge of the Classics is
a real safeguard. When Latin was a second
mother-tongue common to all educated people
in all nations, international relations were easier

than they are now, because to all alike, what was said or written in Latin conveyed the same meaning. But, even now, a classical education remains a source of mutual understanding which is of very great value. Those who have shared it have an added power of getting their minds alongside of one another. Their mechanism is set to the same wave-length.

Now, that common basis was once confined to a small number of people, belonging roughly and in the majority to what might be called a governing class. It came to be regarded, both inside and outside of that circle, as a class-badge. Hence the prejudice against a classical education as undemocratic. But if a democracy is to fulfil its purpose, if it is to rise to its responsibilities as a nation or as an empire, it must level up, not level down.

Baths were once the appanage of a small social class. That was not remedied by discarding baths, but by bringing them into larger, as nearly as may be into universal use. The Classics are baths for the mind. It is through them, in Arnold's words, that "we know the capabilities and performances of the human spirit."

But more especially, let me revert to the point which I have already emphasised, that this study is not as regards its Imperial function the study of ancient language, and is something even higher than the study of ancient institutions and of the work done, with its lessons of encouragement and warning, with its record of successes and failures, by our predecessors in the movement of civilisation. It is the study of the Classics in the true sense of that word, of the incomparable masterpieces which those predecessors have handed down to us. It is acquaintance with the best that there is in thought and in the expression of thought. It is living in the highest company. It is using our capital to purpose and multiplying our wealth. It is the building up of national and Imperial character.

Let me end by quoting the striking words of the Prime Minister in a speech he made in December last. "The idea of particular people," he said, "pursuing learning has been familiar for scores of centuries, but the idea of preparing the minds of whole classes or communities for co-operation and common action by a training in common ideas is a comparatively new one. That is the gigantic task to which we are committed."

We are committed to it, and it has to be done. It is only to be added that those common ideas can best be impressed and assimilated by making acquaintance with them in their most perfect and most permanent expression. That is what the Classics give us.

# XII

# PATRIOTISM

PRESIDENTIAL ADDRESS TO THE CLASSICAL ASSOCIATION
OF SCOTLAND, AT GLASGOW, MARCH 7, 1925.

I WILL not waste many words in expressing my
sense of the honour the Association has done me
in inviting me to fill their Presidential Chair this
year. But I may be allowed to say this; that
while for such an office some, indeed many, of
your own members, of those now engaged, or
who have been engaged for a lifetime, in the
direct conduct of classical studies in Scotland,
have high and just claims, the new departure
recently taken in electing to it, from time to time,
others from outside of your own working and
fighting ranks seems to me in every way com-
mendable and likely to enhance the prestige, to
enlarge the sphere, and to increase the effective-
ness of the Association's work by bringing it into
closer relationship with the larger life of the
nation. Our studies are no more free than any
other studies from the risk of becoming narrowed
and professionalised. It may help us materially
both towards a fuller sense of their scope and
value, and towards their pursuit in a spirit of
faith and hope—I might add, perhaps, or might
twenty or thirty years ago have been inclined to
add, of charity—if we call in a marked way for

the co-operation of those who, though not sharing directly in the work of the Association and of the greater number of its members, are nevertheless in sympathy with its aims and objects; who recognise the value of the Classics in action, the enrichment which has been derived from the Classics in their own education and in their subsequent career, the abiding foundations which the Classics lay for the life .of the citizen and the human being.

The English Classical Association numbers among its past Presidents not only scholars of professional distinction and teachers of long experience, but statesmen, administrators, artists, men of science, men of affairs. The list includes a Prime Minister, a President of the Royal Society, a Lord Chancellor, a chairman of one of the great banks. If, or so far as, it remains true that it is Scotsmen who govern the United Kingdom and the Empire, this Association should in time be able to show no less distinguished a list, and may extend its prerogative still further by the accession to that list of captains of industry or commerce, and of leaders of labour. Our gospel, the faith of the Classics, has to be preached to every creature, without distinction of class or calling. It offers spiritual, not material wealth; and that wealth is not only individual, but national. I need not remind you that it was the old and admirable Scottish education, based largely on the Classics and informed throughout by the classical temper, which gave Scotland its place in the world.

The resolution then, adopted unanimously by th e Association two years ago, that the Presidency

Q

should be offered to a non-professional scholar distinguished in public life, seems well calculated to further its purpose; and with the further experimental and provisional decision that it should be an annual office I should like to say that I am also in full sympathy. The more permanent office of Chairman of Executive serves to ensure continuity of guidance. A succession of Presidents chosen from the widest field, and standing aside from the technicalities and the controversies— these last sometimes needless and always uncomfortable—of educational machinery, can, as it seems to me, do much to secure the requisite breadth of interest and largeness of outlook which the study of the Classics, as an element in the formation of national character and the conduct of national affairs, demands. It can do much towards superseding the conflict of sectional interests, and transforming hindrances into helps, the stifling weight of machinery into the organic movement of life.

When I look to the qualifications set forth by the Association's rule for its future Presidents, I am conscious that I can lay no claim to the qualification of being distinguished in public life. My own life has been mainly passed in the public service; and that is a service which does its work (as no doubt much of the best work is often done) in silence. But I would be the last person to cavil at the liberal extension which the Association has given to this provision.

Lord Finlay, in his address at Edinburgh last year, gave an interesting and eloquent vindication of the importance of the Classics in education. It would be idle to go over the same ground, or to

reiterate the case which he set forth so ably and
persuasively. I wish this afternoon to deal with
an aspect of the Classics, and of their function and
power, which is of much importance, and lies
deep at the foundations of the cause which we
represent. The title chosen may seem perhaps to
have a rather slender connection with the special
work and aims of a Classical Association. But I
trust to be able to convince you—or rather, I hope,
to strengthen your own conviction—that it has
not ; that the connection is, in more ways than one,
intimate and essential.

But I shall not ask you to embark on an un-
charted sea ; and I will therefore attempt briefly
to indicate the distinct but convergent lines of
thought which the subject suggests. To an
audience of my countrymen I need offer no apology
for insisting on the need of a modicum—or may I
say, a sufficiency—of clearness in definition, as
well as of logical sequence in argument. First,
therefore, let me make one point clear. I have
been speaking, and shall be speaking, of the
Classics, not of Latin and Greek. These two
things are different, both in what they include
and what they imply.

Latin and Greek are languages unsurpassed
in many ways, unequalled in several : for accuracy
and precision, for gravity and delicacy, for the
power of saying much in little, and of saying it
perfectly, for logic of structure and beauty of
phrasing. They are languages, Latin more especially, of special value in education, both for mental
discipline and for teaching the principles and
developing the control of language generally. And
language, as I need not remind you, is not only

the mechanism of all thought, the record of all experience, the link between human beings, but is also no less certainly if a little less obviously the motive force which lies behind all creative and all productive work in any association or community. Further, Latin and Greek are the languages which are the keys opening the doors, for an example or warning, of the civilisation out of which our own has in fact arisen. But this is not the point on which I wish to dwell. What I would ask you to consider is not the Latin and Greek languages, nor even the body of Latin and Greek literature. It is the Latin and Greek Classics. It is, that is to say, those works, written in Greek or in Latin, directly accessible to us only through knowledge of these languages, and requiring, in order that they may retain and continue their influence, a perpetual succession secured for transmission of the power to read and appreciate and assimilate them, which are Classics in the full meaning of the word ; which convey to us the best, the highest, the most fruitful human thought as it has received its best and most consummate expression.

The Classics in this sense are not confined to the Greek and Latin Classics alone. There are English, French, Italian Classics. There are, we may claim with modest pride, our own Scottish Classics. But the Greek and Latin Classics have such a primacy, such a settled supremacy, such a depth and fullness of vital meaning accumulated round them and remaining unbroken after standing the test of between two and three thousand years that it is they and they alone which we primarily think of and speak of by

that name. To them we perpetually return, year
after year in our own life, age after age in the life
of mankind ; finding them, with added experience,
always even greater than we had known.

Let me borrow here a familiar phrase from a
small native Classic of our own, from the Shorter
Catechism. The question, What is the meaning,
the use, the value of the Classics as a national
study and an element in the life of the Commonwealth ? might be put in the form, What do the
Classics principally teach ? And it might be
answered, for my present purpose—for other
purposes other answers might no doubt be given
—What man is to believe concerning patriotism,
and what duty patriotism requires of man.

It may be well at this point to define patriotism
a little more clearly, and to attach an agreed
meaning to a word often abused or vaguely used.
Once this meaning, with its different aspects or
implications, has been laid down with approximate
accuracy, we shall be better able to approach the
two main heads of this discourse, that is to say,
what the Classics give and what they ask in
return : first, the effect of the Classics, the virtue
of the Classics, in creating, enlarging, and heighten-
ing patriotism ; and secondly, the patriotism which
the Classics, and the cause which they represent,
claim from us whether as their students or teachers,
or more largely, as their adherents and supporters.

Patriotism is a single thing. But it has different
spheres of action : "there are diversities of opera-
tions, but the same spirit." Originally, a patriot,
*patriotes*, merely meant a fellow-countryman ; that
earlier use survives in the curious word "com-
patriot," which is not, as one might suppose,

a modern coinage, but goes back for more than
three hundred years. It implied nothing more;
and this may remind us that, similarly, the word
"Classic" by etymology merely means "belonging
to a class," and that the meaning "belonging to
the first or highest class" is an accident of later
usage. Up to the early eighteenth century "a
good patriot" was the term that had to be used
to express the further meaning which we now
attach to the word "patriot" alone; and it was
about the same time that the word "patriotism"
seems first to have come into use.

In all its applications, patriotism indicates and
emphasises two things: first, membership of a
community; secondly, devotion to the interest,
the welfare, the service of that community, and
subordination to it of other interests or aims or
advantages, whether they be those of the individual
himself, or of some group or party to which he
belongs. There is a patriotism of the family or
clan, based on ties of blood, or consciousness of
actual kinship and common ancestry. There is a
patriotism of locality of the district or county or
town or even village which has to some extent a
corporate life of its own, a continuity in which it
takes pride, and a sense of neighbourliness based
on neighbourhood. Superior to and including
these, there is national patriotism. Beyond that
we need not now extend our view; though even
beyond it there may be, as an ideal or aspiration,
a wider patriotism of a league or commonwealth
of nations, extending ultimately to such a world-
wide unity as was the dream of the Middle Ages
under the name of the Holy Roman Empire.

Further, one may speak in a quite intelligible

sense of the patriotism of other forms of association to which men belong: the patriotism of a
profession, such as medicine or law, of a religious
community, of a trade union.  There is a patriotism
of our own Association; a devotion to the cause
for which it stands, a loyalty to it as the champion
of that cause, a willing service in promoting its
objects, a subordination to its welfare of individual
predilections or personal advantages.  But it is of
the larger national patriotism, towards which these
others serve or ought to serve, that I ask your
consideration.  To it these minor or sectional
patriotisms are subordinate.  That they should
work in harmony with it and reinforce it is the
ideal still far from being realised, but to be more
and more realised through the instinct for community, the practice of unselfishness, which they
all, in their sphere and their measure, develop and
sustain.

Here I should like to quote some striking words
of the late Joseph Conrad's.  "Patriotism," he said,
"is a somewhat discredited sentiment, because the
delicacy of our humanitarianism regards it as a
relic of barbarism. . . . It requires a certain greatness of soul to interpret patriotism worthily ; or
else a sincerity of feeling denied to the vulgar
refinement of modern thought, which cannot understand the august simplicity of a sentiment pro-
ceeding from the very nature of things and men."
There is nothing to add to this, except that
patriotism, though a sentiment, is something more
and higher than a sentiment: and is wholly free
from sentimentalism.  It is a controlling, inspiring,
exalting force.  It implies, as Conrad says, not
only sincerity of feeling, but greatness of soul.

It is in Greece and Rome, as they are interpreted
and recorded for us in the Greek and Latin Classics,
that this greatness of soul is most conspicuous. It
is there that the clearest lessons, the most noble
examples of patriotism are still to be found. They
begin, in their full splendour, with the immortal
passages or single lines in the *Iliad* like Hector's
incomparable reply to the caution of Polydamas
that the omens are against them and they may die
on the field—it comes exactly at the central point
of the *Iliad*—"One omen is best, to defend the
Fatherland." They end, in the dusk of the Roman
Empire, with the words of the Emperor Valentinian
when calling up his son, still little more than a
boy, to share, not the pomp of an Imperial Court,
but the *augustum commilitium*, the fellowship of
a sacred service. You may read the words in
Ammianus Marcellinus, the last, or all but the
last, of the Latin Classics: "To expose his life for
the companions of his dangers, to love the Republic
as though it were his father's house, to endure
sun and frost, thirst and night-watches, to spend
his blood and breath deliberately for the salvation of the Roman Empire." They are like the
words in which, 1500 years later, Garibaldi led
out his followers from the Rome that he had not
saved by his soldiership into the Italy that he was
to redeem and recreate by his example, and in
which there is the echo of that ancient patriotism
in language little removed from that of the Romans
of old. "Non offro nè paga, nè quartiere, nè
provvigioni: offro fame, sete, marcie forzate, bat-
taglie e morte. Chi ha il nome d'Italia non sulle
labbre soltanto ma nel cuore, mi segua." "I offer
neither pay nor quarters nor provisions: I offer

hunger, thirst, forced marches, battles, and death.
Let him who has the name of Italy in his heart
and not on his lips only, follow me."

In historic Greece, the Greece of the great
Greek Classics, the patriotism of the city-state
reached its highest point and received its most
memorable expression. It took substance in
many conspicuous examples; but more largely
still, in the massed,' or one might almost say the
communised patriotism which made Athens, in
the most brilliant period of its own or of any
recorded human history, unparalleled. I need
not recall, they need no recalling, the names
hardly even now to be read or spoken without a
thrill, of Marathon and Salamis; nor the epitaphs
of Simonides, nor the Funeral Speech of Pericles.
In these, what is to be noted is the simplicity of
the words expressing an equal simplicity of
thought, of faith and purpose; a belief so naturally
grasped that it can hardly be spoken of as an ideal;
a devotion so instinctive that it has not to be
argued, pleaded for, praised, defended, but only
to let itself be felt. It is no idle superstition or
weak idolatry that kindles to and almost worships
the name of Athens. For we feel that in it, as its
spirit is embodied in the Greek Classics, we are
presented not so much with the virtue or genius
of individuals as with an inspiration from above
which descended on the whole nation and made
it greater than any of the individuals who composed it; the sense of community, of membership
in one body, overbearing the individualism, the
sectionalism, the greed or selfishness, the timidity
or jealousy, to which as individuals they were no
less prone than any other men.

You will remember the story of Aristides:
accepting the decree of exile passed on him at the
instance of the democratic party; thinking in his
banishment of nothing but the good of Athens
and the cause of Greek unity; coming, on the
night before Salamis, threading his way in the
dark through the Persian fleet, to bring intelligence of vital importance to his successful rival,
Themistocles; and thereafter devoting all his
energies to co-operation in the national cause
with his old political opponents and to bringing
his own party into line in the conduct of the war,
and, after victory, in the task of reconstruction.
Aristides was called "the just." What he did, all
Athenians knew they ought to do. With all their
faults—their impulsiveness, their passion for
talking, their fits of childishness and savagery—
they did really merge their own life in that of
Athens.

In the Latin Classics we find the precepts and
the examples of a patriotism inspired by a like
devotion, but confirmed in a more binding tradition and applied on a larger scale. Roman
patriotism began where Greek patriotism ended,
in being civic. But it went further; it had the
strength to do this, because it was so built up and
buttressed on sacredness of custom and no less
on sacredness of law. The city grew into a nation,
the nation into an empire. For long, the sense
of patriotism expanded with that growth. Not
until it at last grew weak did Rome begin to decay.
No more than other communities was Rome free
from the selfishness of privileged and the dis-
content of unprivileged classes, from wrecking
demagogues and obstinate reactionaries. But no

other city or nation has so splendid and continuous a record of citizens who subordinated everything, wealth, power, office, the interest of their own class, life itself, and what was dearer still, the life of their children, to the service of the Republic, to the national ideal. Patriotism was with them less a passion than a law. It is put with the incomparable Roman brevity in the maxim laid down by Cicero as the central rule to be observed by all those who for their term of office were invested with the *imperium*, the delegated sovereignty of the Roman people, *Salus populi suprema lex esto*. In that maxim they rose to the conception of a law beyond law; and they carried it out in practice. Their fundamental principle of the sovereignty of the people did not make them hesitate in creating, and using when need arose, the device of the dictatorship; supreme power, military and civil, over the whole magistracy and the whole commonwealth conferred on a single citizen for a fixed period and for a prescribed purpose. It is the most striking testimony to the patriotism both of the Roman people and of individual citizens, that no abuse was ever made of this absolute power; that the dictator always laid down his office as soon as he had finished the special task assigned to him; and that only once was an ex-dictator called on to answer for alleged misconduct. That dictator was the great Camillus. He was accused of having made an unfair distribution of the plunder after the capture of Veii. Popular feeling ran so strongly against him that he left Rome and went into voluntary exile. Within a few months, the Gauls invaded Latium, crushed the Roman army sent out to meet them,

and occupied and burned Rome itself. Without
hesitation, Camillus was in his absence appointed
dictator a second time. With as little hesitation
he accepted the office, collected a force, and
surprised and routed the Gallic army. He re-
entered Rome in triumph, saluted by the crowds
as "father of his country," took order for the
restoration of the burned temples, and laid down
his dictatorship.

One may be reminded of Aristides. But there
is this difference, that the action of Aristides was
regarded as something very remarkable; that of
Camillus, as simply the fulfilment of plain ordinary
duty. It is only one among a hundred instances
of the unselfconscious Roman patriotism, which
by tradition and habit was a second nature. No
Roman citizen received, as Aristides did, the name
of "the just." That was taken for granted.
Neither Camillus then, nor Cincinnatus called
from the plough to be consul and dictator and
returning to the plough when he had executed his
office, nor Fabricius, who refused all rewards for
his immense services in the Pyrrhic War, and died
as poor as he had lived, leaving nothing, was
considered as having done anything out of the
way. They had simply done their duty as children
of the Fatherland and citizens of the Republic.
They had been Romans worthy of Rome. They
did not seek praise; that only came to them from
posterity. It would be our dishonour, not theirs,
if we allowed them to fall out of remembrance.
It would be our loss—how great and how wanton!
—if we forgot the standard set for our own conduct
by the plain-living, little-talking, high-thinking
Roman citizen. One of the advantages we have

over our predecessors in the world is that we
have more history behind us. But what good is
that, if we wilfully neglect it ? if we let it disappear
from the nurture of the people ?

No one surely can fail to have his patriotism
heightened, his sense of the greatness of human
nature and the supremacy of civic duty quickened
and exalted for life, who has been enabled to read
of those men in their own language: who has
stored within—to take but two instances—the
Ode of Horace which tells of the Consul Regulus
counselling the Senate never to submit to national
dishonour by making an ignominious peace, and
then quietly returning to certain torture and death
in Carthage because the Roman word might not
be broken: or the noble ending of the sixth
*Aeneid*, where Virgil, as has been finely said,
"sums up in lines like bars of gold the hero-roll
of the Eternal City, conferring with every word
an immortality": or, better still, who has read at
large in the History of Livy, told as it is there
with the noblest eloquence, the age-long record of
Roman patriotism, inherited and transmitted, un-
touched by disgrace, victorious over death.

The greatest thing ever said about Roman
patriots is what was put by Milton in the mouth
of the Son of God Himself:

> Among the heathen canst thou not remember
> Quintius, Fabricius, Curius, Regulus?
> *For I esteem those names.*

Courage, persistence, self-sacrifice—not the thea-
trical self-sacrifice which is only a subtle form of
self-seeking, and is useless to the Commonwealth
—these were the notes of Roman patriotism. It

was not sentimental.  It was not, as we say,
imaginative.  It never lost sight of good sense.
One striking instance, however familiar, may be
aptly recalled.

At Cannae, the greatest Roman army ever
until then put in the field had been out-generalled,
out-fought, and utterly destroyed by Hannibal.
Both consuls were in joint command.  Lucius
Aemilius Paulus, against whose judgment the
battle had been fought, refused to leave the field
with the wreck who escaped.  He preferred, he
said, to die with his men : *bene mori quam turpiter
vivere maluit.*  He sat down by the roadside, and
let himself be killed by the pursuing cavalry.
Gaius Terentius Varro, his colleague, on whom
the responsibility for the battle and the disaster
primarily rested, made good his own escape with
a small force to Venusia, where he collected and
reorganised the wreck of the army.  To Paulus
no praise was given, no posthumous honour paid ;
his death, however heroic, was prodigal (that is
the word used of it long afterwards by Horace) :
it was the useless loss of a Roman life.  Varro
was removed from his command.  But on his
return to Rome, the whole city poured out to
meet him, and he was publicly thanked *quod de re
publica non desperasset.*  To despair of the Republic
was the one failure that could not be allowed, that
could hardly be forgiven.

It was this common national instinct and tradition of patriotism which made Rome great.
Such a spirit prevailing the whole community has
been reached, among many nations and at many
periods of history, in times of war-emergency and
of obvious public danger.  The distinction of

Rome lay in the constancy with which the national spirit was carried through in ordinary civil life, in the pursuits, and the controversies, of peace. The Republic was, through force of circumstances, engaged in frequent, one might almost say in incessant, wars. But the state of war was always regarded as anomalous. There was not until late in Roman history any standing army. In Rome itself, except under a dictatorship, the civil power was supreme, and the legions were not allowed even to enter the city. The force behind the Government was not the sword, but the common patriotism of the citizens. If occasionally it bent under the strain, it did not break; it always recovered itself. During the long constitutional struggles of the first two centuries of the Republic there were repeated general strikes—the famous secessions of the plebs. But they never came to riot or bloodshed; and the last of them issued in a permanent reconciliation. The term "permanent" is, in history, of course, relative; in this case it meant the national concord of 150 years.

This is the standard of patriotism which the Greek and Latin Classics hold up to us, expressing it in language which, in a famous phrase, "has put off flesh and blood and is become immutable." It may be one of the first aims of our Association to expound it, to spread it, to enforce it: and in particular, to impress on the public consciousness that nurture in that high atmosphere should be a widespread national possession; not the study of a select few, not the class-badge of an intellectual aristocracy, but placed within the reach, and pressed on the acceptance, of the whole educated community.

This may perhaps be thought a vague ideal or an impracticable vision. Can it be translated into more definite terms and harnessed to action? I think it can: I will venture to name, and invite you to consider, two definite things that can be worked for and that are not beyond possibility of attainment. Whether or not they will carry your assent, whether or not you will think them things worth fighting for and things for the sake of which other efforts may for the time be postponed, I place them before you. There can at least be no doubt about their meaning. They are these:

(1) That in all Secondary Schools, Latin should be taught as an integral and organic element in the curriculum, not to a few picked boys or girls, but to the whole body of the pupils.

(2) That in the course of study for the Arts Degree at the Universities, Latin should similarly be an integral and indispensable subject.

If you concentrate on these two things—the former of which is, I think, the more vital, and the key to the whole position, though the two will react on one another and are really inseparable—you will for the moment have to let Greek take care of itself. It can: though that does not relieve us from the duty of taking care of it. But about the best thing we can do for the study of Greek at the present moment is to lay firm foundations for it. And those who know Latin will wish to learn Greek; demand will create supply. Further, if you concentrate on these two things, you will not disperse your energies over the invention and elaboration of substitutes, which is always a doubtful and dangerous course to embark upon.

Is the Association prepared to work for securing these two things? I do not wish to thrust them on you as a prescription; I lay them before you as a suggestion. But to ask whether you are prepared to work for the object at which they aim, in this way or in a better if there be one—and I do not myself think that there is a better—is in effect to ask you, do you believe in the Classics? Faith without works, the Apostle tells us, is dead. And work without faith is lifeless. To any one of us, the highest tribute that can be paid at the end of our day is, " Seest thou how faith wrought with his works, and by works was faith made perfect ? "

This has led us to the second head of the subject. If the Classics have taught or helped to teach us patriotism, what special patriotic duty do we owe to the Classics? What are we called on to do, whether as members of the teaching profession, or as more largely interested in education, for the studies which we value and cultivate? Here we may have regard, on the one hand, to the welfare, the culture, the standard of intellectual and spiritual life of Scotland; on the other hand to the community with which each one of us as an individual is more specially related, whether locally, or in relation to other forms of association and common action, a profession or business or industry or trade union. For all such associations alike, what is important is that they should do their own business, and that in doing it they should be inspired by the same patriotic spirit, by pursuit of high ideals and subordination of purely selfish or sectional interests to the larger cause, that of human life. There need be no conflict

R

between the lesser and the larger patriotism if both are, as they ought to be, varying actions or embodiments of the same spirit. Theoretic conflict between one and another patriotic duty may arise. But if the moving spirit be truly patriotic in each case, it is wonderful how seldom there need be doubt as to the right thing to do. All that is needed beyond that spirit is intelligence; and intelligence is just what study of the Classics, if properly pursued by sound methods under skilled guidance, develops and strengthens.

May I be allowed to pursue this part of the subject very briefly into some of its applications?

One of the most important functions of a Classical Association is to strengthen among all its own members the sense of community. It should have this as a conscious object; it should work towards it quietly and steadily. To any one who is an isolated classical teacher in a school, or an isolated student of the Classics, it is a great thing that he should feel himself in touch with colleagues, not ploughing a lonely furrow. Commerce with the greatest minds and the greatest accomplishments of mankind is helped by commerce with others who have like interests, who come to drink at the same fountain. The record of this Association may in this respect be capable of enlargement. Much is to be hoped from the further development of local centres, a work which has been, I am glad to hear, successfully done in some districts : there should be a network of these all over Scotland. Informal meetings of these local branches or centres of groups, and joint meetings with groups interested in other studies —history and literature and philosophy and archae-

ology and the whole circle of the arts and sciences
—cannot be too much encouraged. It is only thus
that interest in our own studies can be widely
extended, and stimulus both given and received.
To effect this means work, and work depends
on enthusiasm. The enthusiasm can be widely
kindled if each member of the Association realises
his or her duty towards it and towards the cause
which it represents. The work may be laborious,
the results may be very gradual. But it is
patriotic work; and it will not be fruitless.

It is no less a patriotic duty to increase our
membership, so that there may be visible proof
of large public support to our cause. We shall
rally this support if we have, and impress on
others, the conviction that the Classics are not
merely a discipline, but a food; that they teach
virtue, that they exalt citizenship, that they connect
our lives with the life of the human race.

A man's foes shall be they of his own household. Scholars are not immune from human
defects and frailties. There are, as there have
been and no doubt will be, among them such
things as pedantry, exclusiveness, arrogance, failure
in a sense of proportion both within the range of
their own studies and as regards the relation of
these studies to others. Even within an organised
association such as this one of ours, there is sometimes less sense than there might be of common
interest, of actual fellowship and co-operation.
Patriotism tells us not to quarrel, not to complain,
not to yield to discouragement or apathy. This
is an imperfect world. We must make the best of
it; and that is exactly what patriotism teaches us
to do. And the Classics have somehow failed in

their effect on us, unless they have not only disciplined our minds as instruments, but humanised our conduct in social life; unless they have bred in us their own spirit, the spirit summed up in the magnificent words, *Qui sponte obtulistis animas vestras, benedicite Domino.* That is what they can give: that it is our own fault if they do not give, alike by the splendour of the ideals they present and by the example of the achievements they record.

To know the great Classics—Homer, Thucydides, Plato, Livy, Virgil—is a privilege which may fall to the lot of few. To know even a little of them, to get glimpses into the world which they open up, may be brought within the reach of many. To know that such a world exists and is within reach, to be conscious of it by faith (which is the evidence of things not seen), to have the chance of entering into it, might be so general as to be almost universal. National patriotism and an educated nation are the two sides of the same shield. Education founded on patriotic purpose and carried on in a patriotic spirit is the national structure which we, like our colleagues in other quarters of the field—in science, art, economics, industry—are concerned with building up.

This, too, may be said as a last word about patriotism, that while it requires guarding and fostering, while it may decay from neglect or be distorted by misusage, it is deeply rooted in human nature, and is not dead even where it seems to have fallen asleep. It cannot be killed either by false teaching or by bad example. One hears much of the selfishness of individual against individual, of class against class, even of study

against study.  Of the patriotism which, in the
greater and in the lesser spheres alike, acts constantly as a bond of union, we hear little.  It does
not strive or cry.  It is hardly conscious of itself.
But it is there: sometimes to manifest itself
amazingly in great emergencies, always to keep
the frame of society together.  Patriotism, devotion to the *patria*, would be a meaningless word if
there were no *patria*, no community and common
good, to be devoted to.  It means the sense and
the assurance of kinship.  Kinship is the same
word as kindness.  Kindness is the same thing as
love.  Love is the ultimate motive force of the
world.

THE END